ART AND HISTORY
VENICE

E-mail: bonechi@bonechi.it

The text of the historical introduction to Venice and the description of monuments were written by *Nino Cenni* for "Veneto Paese per paese", published by our Publishing House.

ISBN-10: 88-476-2093-7
ISBN-13: 978-88-476-2093-3

Printed in Italy by *Centro Stampa Editoriale Bonechi.*

Translation: *Erika Pauli, Studio Comunicare,* Firenze

The photographs belong to the archive of *Casa Editrice Bonechi* and were taken by:
Paolo Giambone, Gaetano Barone, Gianni Dagli Orti.
Photographs kindly provided by the *Azienda di Promozione Turistica di Venezia*, and taken by *Renato Boscolo*: pages 87, 97c.
Aerial photographs *I-BUGA* - Aut. SMA n. 506/85: pages 19, 85, 103, 108.

The publisher apologizes for any omissions and is willing to make amends with the formal recognition of the author of any photo subsequently identified.

Internet: www.bonechi.com

INTRODUCTION

Water-girt Venice rises on an archipelago of small islands separated by a dense network of waterways, which were rectified as time passed, noticeably changing the original conformation. Venice lies four kilometers from the mainland and two from the open sea. The original inhabited nucleus of the city took shape during the barbarian invasions when groups of refugees from Spina, Aquileia, Adria, Altino, Padua settled on the islands in the lagoon. In the course of the centuries the population kept increasing, developing into a city the likes of which is not to be found anywhere in the world.
It must also be kept in mind that since over 160 waterways have been covered with earth, the number of islands on which Venice stands has been reduced to eighteen, inclusive of San Giorgio Maggiore and the Giudecca.
The longest of the canals (3.8 km.) and the widest (from 30 to 70 m.) is the Grand Canal which divides the city into two parts that are interconnected by three bridges: the Bridge of the Scalzi, the Bridge of Rialto and that of the Accademia. Forty-five rii or internal canals run into the Grand Canal and they can all be navigated with small boats or gondolas. As many as 450 bridges connect the various zones of the city. The territory is subdivided into sestrieri or districts: Cannaregio, San Marco, Castello, Dorsoduro, San Polo, Santa Croce. Until 1480 the bridges were in wood; later they were replaced by arched stone structures.
Land travel moves over spaces that have their own specific names.
There are not many main streets, rughe (from the French rue) and the salizade or first streets in the city to be paved (selciate). The smaller alleys are called cale or calle while those that run close to the canals and serve as foundations for the houses are known as fondamenta; the lista is that stretch of road next to an embassadorial residence which enjoyed a particular diplomatic immunity. In addition there are the mercerie, streets lined by shops of various kinds, the rive which are stretches of fondamenta along the rii, the smaller waterways, and more specifically the steps which lead to the water from the fondamenta. Rii tera are filled-in canals, the rami are short stretches of road that branch off from a calle or a campiello. The campo is the square near a church, a large area of open ground once cultivated, mostly as a vegetable garden or used to pasture horses. The campiello is the smaller open space between the houses, to which the calli lead. The small open areas surrounded by buildings and with only one entrance/exit are known as corti. Paludo is the name given to those spaces where there was once a swamp (palude) while the pissine are in the sites of pools where it was possible to fish and swim. What else makes Venetian toponomy unique and an abbreviated survey of history and town-planning? The sotoportego, a stretch of road that passes under the buildings and connects calli, campielli, corti... and then the « canals », water-ways, but not by any means minor « ways » of communication — Anything but...!
On the same level as the toponomy, telling the tale of the town- planning history of the city, but the bane of anyone who is not a born Venetian, are the house numbers. The houses are progressively numbered, but according to district and not distinguished into calli, campi, campielli... It was this need to put some order into the confused state of affairs in the city that led to an initial regular numbering of the houses in 1801. This was not however progressive for sestieri, but for the zona de citra and de ultra, on this side and that of San Marco, so that the zone of de citra includes Castello, San Marco and Cannaregio and de ultra Santa Croce, Dorsoduro and San Polo. Between 1837 and 1941 a survey by districts was instituted and the « black numbers » were replaced by « red » ones. Even so, in certain areas of Venice it is still possible to see examples of « local » numbers in Roman numerals next to the regular numbers in Arab numbers. And sometimes the Roman numerals are written backwards, as in the sotoportego degli Armeni at St. Mark's, where the house numbers 963-964 on one building are flanked by the letters IIIIV and IIIV which stand for IX and VIII.
Basically Venice today still looks as it did in the 13th century, with the exception of a few transformations in various buildings which however play an unimportant part in the general layout of the city plan.
It was not until the 19th century that the need to facilitate communications with the Mainland, and the constant growth in population, led to a few particularly important changes. Connections with the Mainland in fact improved and were speeded up thanks to the construction of the railroad bridge (1841-46) which with its 3,601 meters joins water-girt Venice to Mestre. The road bridge, opened almost a century later, in 1933, now also makes it possible to reach the Mainland by car.
Insular Venice covers an area of a little over seven square kilometers, inclusive of the islands of San Giorgio and the Giudecca.
The area that falls under the jurisdiction of the Commune of Venice is much larger, comprising other important inhabited centers: the islands of Murano, Burano and Torcello, inside the lagoon, the Lido and Pellestrina towards the sea, Malcontenta, Dese, Tessera, Mestre and Marghera, Zelarino, Carpenedo, Asseggiano, Trivignano, Favaro and Chirignago in the immediate hinterland. Some of these places were once autonomous communes.

HISTORY OF VENICE

A history of Venice infers a starting point. But what about « pre-Venice »? What changes of fortune characterized the lives of the peoples who then came to settle the Venetian lagoons in the early centuries of the Christian era?
It is extremely difficult if not impossible to know with precision what happened, but it does seem to be possible to trace back the existence of Veneto populations to even earlier than the reference to be found in Titus Livius to the « subtle shores and pools » and the men who lived there in 302 B.C. and dispersed the fleet of Cleonemes, son of the king of Sparta.
The archaeological finds from the Euganean Hills, the plateau of Asiago, the areas around Verona and Trieste tell us that human settlements had already existed for a long time around the lagoons and in the interior. The ancestors of the refugees of Altino were most probably the pile dwellers of the Venetian lakes and marshes. This technique of building on piles, upon which the most important monuments of Venice also rest, has remained unchanged throughout the centuries. The *casoni* of the centuries of Atestine culture also went up on the reclaimed « subtle shores and on the pools », with a building technique that only the use of stone was to change.
Those who lived on the small poor islands in the lagoon were also Veneto populations, people who may have lived at the margins of civilization and the splendors of Rome while not far off Oderzo, Concordia, Altino, Padua and Aquileia were being settled. The beginnings of Aquileia, a river port and important road junction, date to 181 B.C. It was also an outpost, in the early centuries after Christ, against the threat of the Quadi, the Marcomanni and the Sarmations who were crowding down into the Veneto, the beginning of a long period of invasions from the north and east, followed by the Alamanni, Alaric's Goths, and finally the Swabian Vandals and the Alans. The last invader was Attila at the head of his Huns, leaving such destruction in his wake as to merit the name of the « scourge of God ».
It was during these years that Venice was born.
The traditional date for the birth of the Serenissima is March 25, 421. This seems to be when the first stone of the church of San Giacometto was placed (actually 11th cent.). In any case, the real beginnings of Venice were when under the menace of the Barbarians the inhabitants of the Veneto-Roman cities sought refuge in the huts of the salters, vegetable gardeners and fishermen, built in the marshes of the lagoon. The same thing must have happened again in 452 with the invasion of Attila's Huns who burned Aquileia and devastated Altino and Concordia Sagittaria despite their strong defenses.
In 466 the representatives of the communities which had settled the islands in the lagoon met in Grado to choose a type of government, and the two tribunes, elected annually in every community, remained the highest authorities until the advent of the dogate. Acknowledgement of the state of affairs in the Veneto lagoon, characterized not only by the presence of populations but also by economic activity, is forthcoming from an official document of 523 written by Cassiodorus, minister to Theodoric, who had turned to the military-tribunes in order to get help from those sea- farers in transporting foodstuffs from Istria, because of the famine which had struck all of northern Italy. And since Cassiodorus was also a good writer, his letter provides us with important information on the tides, navigation in the waterways and the putting out to sea of the boats, together with the first recognition of the marine power of « Venetia » that was then in the process of being formed.
The Gotho-Byzantine war which broke out in 535 and which aimed at recuperating all of the north and Italy for the Roman Empire of the East, saw the presence of Venetian ships on the side of Constantinople. In 539 Ravenna, the capital, was blockaded, and the ships of those who were then to become Venetians were there. In 551 once more the Veneto ships collaborated in transporting the troops of Narsetes and legend says that as a sign of gratitude he then founded the churches of SS. Geminiano and Menna and of San Teodoro in Piazza San Marco. Later Venetian tradition interpreted this aid to Constantinople as a political move, conceived of in terms of parity, and the chronicles of Altino in the 12th century already exalt the independence of the Veneto. Even though it actually consisted of normal aid supplied to the legitimate government by a loyal city of the imperial province, it should be stressed that while independence may not be implied, it did on the other hand imply the recognition by Constantinople of how fundamentally important the Venetian navy was in the difficult waters of the lagoon and the upper Adriatic.
The Byzantine empire however could do nothing to halt the conquest of the lands north of the lagoon by the Lombards who came down into Italy in 568 with Alboin, and fugitives fleeing from the dominion of these new conquerors continued to arrive in the islands. It was a migration not only of families, but also of entire organized groups which found refuge in Grado, Torcello, Chioggia, Caorle, Malamocco, Albiola, Poveglia and the islands which form Venice, where a settlement was already recorded in Olivolo, the island which was to be called Castello, after the fort that may have been built there as early as Roman times.
In 640 when Oderzo, the capital of the province, fell to the Lombards, a new city that was to take its place was officially born in the middle of the Venetian lagoons. This new capital « Città Nuova » was also called Eracliana and Eraclea in honor of the Byzantine emperor of the time, Heracleonas. Cittanova has disappeared and its original site has only recently been identified.
The islands of the lagoon, in other words, became ever more populated, with stable residential centers, despite the fact that they were not exactly ideal for comfortable living.
In 639 the cathedral dedicated to Mary was founded on Torcello where a community that originally came from Altino lived. On the document of its foundation — which still exists — are to be found the names of Isaac and Mauricius, respectively exarch of Ravenna and « magister militum », which testifies to the administrative bonds between the lagoon community and Byzantium. The other bishop's seat on the lagoon was in Grado, where the patriarch of Aquileia had found refuge. This diocese, said to be founded by Saint Mark and second only to Rome, was transferred to Grado during the so-called « schism of the three capitals » and even as it was born the lagoon was witness to the sowing of the seeds of the future religious tensions with the Church.
Thus, while Eraclea was the administrative center, Grado the religious seat, and Torcello the most prosperous island economically speaking, the communities on the lagoon were completely lacking in unity and internal contrasts were inevitable. Legend narrates that the first « *dux* » (which later became doge in the Venetian dialect), a superior authority for the entire lagoon, was elected in Cittanova in 697.
The legend also says that his name was Paoluccio Anafesto and that he was elected by twelve old families: Badoer, Barozzi. Contarini, Dandolo, Falier, Gradenigo, Memmo, Michiel, Morosini, Tolani, Sanudo and Tiepolo. Giovanni Diacono in the 11th century affirms that at the time of King Luitprand, elected in 712, Duke Paulicius and the *magister militum* together defined the borders of the province in the territory of Cittanova. But while the existence of any kind of pact with Luitprand appears highly improbable, it is clear that « Paulicius » and Marcello could be no other than magistrates

of the Byzantine army charged with tracing the frontier with the Lombard territory, and a Paul was exarch of Ravenna from 723 to 727. Apparently the first historical « *dux* » then can be identified with the Ursus who took command of the lagoons in 727, head of the soldiers in the rebellion against the iconoclastic decree of Leo III the Isaurian, a general revolt against the destruction of the sacred images that was upheld by the Church of Rome. A few years later this same Ursus received the title of « *hypatos* » (consul) from Byzantium, which was then transformed by his descendants into the surname Ipato.

The authority of Byzantium was however on the wane: in 742 Orso's son Teodato took over power and transferred the capital to Malamocco, which was already to all extents and purposes the capital of an autonomous state. In the course of the 8th century the colonization of the islands around Rialto began. They were safer because of the shallow shoals but this also made them more subject to the dangers of the tides. A complicated period in the life of the lagoon began in 764 with Doge Maurizio Galbaio.

FROM THE NINTH TO THE TWELFTH CENTURY

When the pope, who had had Rome, Spoleto, the Marches and the Exarchate itself as far as the Paduan delta given him, called in the Franks, in 766 the Roman Curia obtained Maritime Venice and Istria. In different historical situations the lagoons moreover were later to witness the clash between the Franks and the Papacy in which the occasionally ambiguous action of the patriarch of Grado played an important role. Nor, to be honest, did the doges themselves succeed in choosing better positions, and it got to the point where the Franks decided to occupy the entire Veneto territory. But when Pepin, at the head of the attacking forces, reached the port of Albiola and tried to penetrate the waters of the lagoon, the Frankish fleet was hindered in its manoeuvres and was repulsed. The canal where the Venetians massacred the Franks is still called Canale Orfano. After this episode, the government decided to move to Rivoalto, and laid the foundations for the future development of the city. In 831 the body of Saint Mark was brought to Venice by Rustico da Torcello and Bon da Malamocco. In order to house the mortal remains with fitting dignity it was decided to build a church next to the Doges' Palace. In the meanwhile Venice kept growing and the « Pactum Lotharii », stipulated by Doge Pietro Tradonico with the emperor to defend the city from the aggressions of the Slavs, lists the places which at the time belonged to the duchy: Rialto, Olivolo, Murano, Malamocco, Albiola, Chioggia, Brondolo, Fossone, Loreo, Torcello, Ammiana, Burano, Cittanova, Fine, Equilio, Caorle, Grado and Cavarzere. The borders, in other words, arrived only as far as the « *aquas salsas* ». Mestre, Campalto and Tessera therefore were not part of the duchy. The pact was renewed in 880 and this time it was worded in such a way that it read as a pact stipulated specifically between the emperor and the doge and no longer between the Venetians and their neighbors.

In 889 the Hungarians attempted to take over the lagoonal islands, but they were defeated by Doge Pietro Tribuno. Aware of the danger Venice was subject to from the sea, he had a great wall built that began at the castle of Olivolo, and reached all the way to Santa Maria del Giglio where a large chain was stretched, in case of danger, from near the church of San Gregorio up to Dorsoduro. Another problem was represented by the Istrian pirates who imperilled the Venetian merchants. The situation was resolved in the agreement of Capodistria of 932 signed by Pietro II Candiano who also led the war against Comacchio, which threatened the Venetian monopoly on salt. It was therefore the merchants who determined the political and military choices of the doges, up to the point where a rebellion broke out when Pietro IV Candiano emitted various decrees which preoccupied the world of trade. The Doges' Palace was assaulted and since the soldiers faithful to the doge had barricaded themselves in the palace, the rebels set fire to the neighboring houses to drive them out. The fire damaged more than had been intended, destroying three hundred houses all the way to Santa Maria Zobenigo, and both the Basilica and the Church of San Teodoro burned down. Rebuilding of the city started immediately, aided by the new doge, Pietro Orseolo I, who lavishly gave of his own money and imposed the first « tithe » in Venice to reconstitute the finances of the State. Particularly important for Venice was the reign of Doge Pietro Orseolo II who obtained the *Bolla d'Oro* from the Byzantine emperor in 992, thus ensuring much lower import tariffs for trade goods for Venice, in exchange for aid against the Arabs, than those of their Amalfi, Hebrew and Lombard competitors, as well as permitting the Venetian merchants to account directly to the *logoteta* of Byzantium, freeing them from the graft involved in bureaucracy.

The statues of the Tetrarchs, in red porphyry.

For a certain period of time the contrast between the Patriarchate of Aquileia and that of Grado were in the limelight, for the former was aiming at annexing the latter. An attempt made by Poppone of Aquileia however failed because of the decisive opposition of Doge Ottone Orseolo and the issue was closed in 1043 by Doge Domenico Contarini.

The end of the 11th century was characterized by the battles

Venice had to engage in (above all during the reign of Doge Domenico Selvo) against the Norman advance in the Adriatic. It was in the winter of 1084-85 that the Venetian fleet suffered its first defeat, with the loss of seven ships which sank and the capture of others with their crews.
In the meanwhile in the Holy Land there had been a new wave of Muslim intolerance for Venice, forced to approach the area with a fleet headed by Giovanni Michiel, a naval force that was to serve as reinforcement for Goffredo di Buglione in his conquest of Haifa. Near Jaffa the Venetian fleet registered an important victory against Byzantium, which refused to respect the privileges of the *Bolla d'Oro*. As a reward for its decisive intervention, in every city in the Realm of Jerusalem, Venice obtained a district with church, mill, press, bakery, bath, square and service of weights and measures, exempt from taxes, duty, visitor's tax, and in addition the privilege of jurisdiction.
While the situation on the seas and in the East was favorable for Venice, problems began to arise on the Mainland, for the new emperor of Germany, Frederick I called Barbarossa, was out to conquer all of Italy. Even so Venice did no more than make a substantial contribution in favor of the Lombard League which opposed him and, then, five years later, even sent her fleet to the aid of the bishop of Mainz in Ancona. It was a move aimed at letting someone besides Frederick Barbarossa win. In the end the emperor and Pope Alexander III met in Venice in 1177; the city, as far as she was concerned, obtained the confirmation of the old pacts and full imperial guaranty of the safety of the Venetian citizens and their holdings throughout the empire; moreover the controversy with Aquileia was settled and Grado extended its see up into Istria and Dalmatia. The city itself was also improved, including the enlargement of the Doges' Palace, as well as of the Piazza and the Piazzetta and the raising of the columns of San Marco and Todaro. In 1187 the peace treaty with Byzantium was signed, with the recognition of Venice's old privileges and with construction for the Byzantine fleet entrusted to the Arsenal. In that same year, 1187, Jerusalem fell into the hands of Saladin, followed by Acre and Laodicea. Upon the pope's request Venice sent a fleet on the Third Crusade but it probably did not fully commit itself. Acre was retaken and new institutional reforms were carried out in Venice, including the creation of the *Procuratori*. It was then that the *Quarantia* (Council of Forty, a sort of supreme tribunal) which had been created previously, was assigned judicial authority. Venice's participation in the Fourth Crusade was just as tepid, a participation whose prime scope was that of using the Crusaders for the destruction of Byzantium, which by then had become an inconvenient ally. The Venetians carried off considerable quantities of art treasures from that city, including the four bronze horses on San Marco and four reliquaries now in the Museo Marciano. In addition, the « *Partitio Romaniae* » turned over the bases of Epirus and the Ionian Islands to the Venetians, a large part of the Peloponnesus, the Aegean Islands and Salamina, the fortresses of Oreòs and Caristo, the Cyclades, the peninsula of Gallipoli and the province of Adrianopolis and Candia. Venice was moreover completely exempted from customs taxes throughout the empire.

COMMERCE, THE MARITIME ROUTES, THE PROFESSIONS

With the *Bolla d'Oro* conceded in 1082 by the Emperor of the East Alexius I Comnenus, the Republic was guaranteed full freedom of trade in the entire territory of the Byzantine Empire. Constantinople itself became the seat of many ship-owners and a great number of merchants.
The development of trade and the constitution of various craft and manufacturing activities was accompanied by an intense immigration into the Venetian isles and at the same time the formation of a moneyed aristocracy that eventually took the power into its own hands.
The Crusades themselves, above all the fourth, gave Venice the opportunity to consolidate her position in the East with the acquisition of various key points for the « commercial » conquest of vast areas. All the goods from northern Italy and eastern Europe headed for the East passed through Venice.
The peril of pirates in the Adriatic, and the convenience of travelling in « escorted » convoys, led to a development of trade in specific periods of the year. At the beginning there were two « *mude* » or convoys: the one from Rumania headed for Constantinople and the one from Cyprus, Lesser Armenia and Syria. Later when Rome revoked the prohibition of trade with Egypt, the *muda* of Alexandria was officially instituted. Beginning in the 14th century, a convoy left Venice once a year for England and Flanders. Thereafter regular services were set up for northwestern Africa and Provence. The armed galleys took it upon themselves to transport the more precious wares — importing pepper, spices, dyes and perfumes, and exporting gold, silver, cloth, wood, tin and iron.
In addition to the *mude* other ships transported goods that were indispensable for life in the city itself or for trade with the neighboring hinterland.
Trade, in other words, was almost the only font of gain Venice had and lay at the basis of the city's constantly growing wealth. The great families never forgot their trade interests and never permitted political power to decree laws that contrasted with their interests.
The oldest form of commercial shop was the *rogadìa* which consisted in acquiring merchandise that was then entrusted to a merchant to be sold in a distant market. In the *colleganza* or *commenda unilaterale* the merchant was entrusted with a certain capital which was returned with the addition of three-quarters of the earnings.
As coinage, from the end of the 12th century on, Venice minted the *grosso d'argento* (two grams and 178 milligrams of silver 968/1000). Business center was Rialto where the office of weights and measures had its headquarters.
Contacts with the East, on the other hand, had led to specialized activities such as those of the jewelers, glass-makers and pharmacists.
Many people also worked at home for the wealthy merchants who distributed the work to be done in the various stages of the production of wool and fustian.
The specific guild organization was involved only in the production of silk. At the turn of the 15th century lace-making also came to the fore.
For the building of ships there was the Arsenal (Dockyard) on the one hand, and the private shipyards, the *squeri* on the other. The Arsenal was charged with seeing to the needs of the military navy while the *squeri* fulfilled the requests of private individuals. The installation of a shipyard had been decided in the 12th century by the Doge Ordelaf Falier and in the beginning it was used above all in the construction of merchant ships. The war against the Turks constrained the Serenissima to fit out a real battle fleet. From the 15th century the *squeraroli* were obliged to lend their services to the Arsenal in case of need. Since the state paid low wages this service was reluctantly provided, at least until the crisis in the shipbuilding sector turned the Arsenal into a « safe haven » for those who preferred sure wages.
As far as the arts and professions were concerned, there were, it is true, some forms of associations in Venice at the beginning of the 11th century, but it must be stressed that it was only much later that the artisans of each sector established precise norms through the institution of associations known also as « *congregationes* » or « *scholae* ». Their scope was purely economical and the life styles they took as models were those of the devotional schools. The statute of each congrega-

tion was also known as « *capitolare* » (chapter) or « *mariegola* ». Each congregation paid directly to the State tributes which were proportional to the income of its members, while the artisans were obliged to offer their services gratuitously to the State. Every association had at its head a *gastaldo* elected from among the most skilled masters. This annual election turned him into a public official, and he could not resign from his office unless he paid a substantial fine.
Not all the arts were open to foreigners. Where it was allowed, the foreigners had to pay a tax called « good entry » (*bona entrada*). Boys could be hired only from the age of twelve up. If the work was particularly heavy this minimum age could be raised. After five or seven years they became workers and after another two or three they could, after a test of their art, become « masters », which was an indispensable qualification for opening a shop of one's own.
The standard with the image of the patron saint, the symbols of the Art or guild, the religious vestments and the coffers of the society were kept in the church or in their official seat where there was always an altar. On the patron saint's feast day there was a procession and after mass was celebrated all the members participated in a banquet. One of the scopes of the Congregations was also that of helping the poor and the sick. This was gradually extended to include pensions for widows, the protection of orphans and the creation of hospitals for sick members.
In a city where for centuries the livelihood of its inhabitants had come from the sea, the fishermen or « *compravendi* » could not escape being the object of particular interest on the part of the government and above all the *Giustizia Vecchia* which set up provisions with regards to just about all the problems, from the types of nets allowed, to the periods in which fishing was permitted, as well as the use of weirs in fishing downstream. The most popular *mariegola* was that of San Nicolò. It should be noted that the fishermen were so important that their chamberlain had the privilege of following the doge with his boat, tieing it to the Bucintoro on the day of the Ascension. The fishermen were prohibited from buying fish caught by others so as to avoid cornering of the market and therefore raising the prices.
Marangoni and *calafati* worked at the Arsenal. The ship *marangoni* could theoretically also work elsewhere but this rarely happened. They contributed to the building of the ships and their headquarters were in SS. Giovanni e Paolo with the Blessed Virgin Mary as their patron saint.
The *calafati d'arsenal* had different headquarters: the patron saints were first Saint Fosca and then Saint Martin. There were *calafatti da 'figger'* (who fixed the planking on the hulls with nails and pins) and « *da maggio* » (who filled the cracks between the planks with cloth). They were not allowed to leave Venice for work without the permission of the doge and had always to take with them the tools of their craft. They could not moreover take on more than one job at a time or work on jobwork. They were also obliged, if necessary. to embark so as to be of aid if the occasion required.
The *peateri* had their headquarters in the church of San Silvestro. A member of the trade had to own his own boat which was never to be left unguarded if it was loaded. In 1553 it was established that only one kind of merchandise at a time could be transported. The boats were not permitted to stop at the Calle dei Botteri and boys under 18 were not allowed to manage them.
Weaving and dying were activities for which the Venetians were justly famous; silk weavers, dyers and linen workers had extremely rigid rules and regulations. Saint Christopher was the patron saint of the silk weavers and the seat was in the Scuola Vecchia of the Misericordia. They were divided into *maestri da pello*, specialized in the weaving of velvet and the *maestri senza pello* specialized in satin.
The *tintori* or dyers had their headquarters first at San Giovanni Crisostomo and then (1581 on) at the Servite church. There were three types of dyers: of cloth, of fustian and of silk. In order to be a dyer one had to have a thorough knowledge of the art of making cloth and this was kept secret by the artisans who were so renowned that in 1532 the queen of France ordered 300 colored satins; Florence itself sent its fabrics to the lagoon to be dyed. The *mariegola* of the guild determined the various substances which could be used and these were of animal origin, such as the kermes from which scarlet was obtained, vegetable such as the *reseda luteola* for yellow, and mineral, such as red hematite from which a special tonality of red was obtained. Kermes came from the Orient but other substances came from the Venetian Mainland. The discovery of America brought new products to Europe and consequently Venice lost its monopoly on the art of dying.
The statute of the *linaroli* or linen workers dates to 1680; their headquarters were in the *fondamenta* of SS. Filippo e Giacomo who, together with Saint Apollonia, were the patron saints. The *linaroli* turned the thread into linen cloth which they could sell either in their own homes or in San Polo on Wednesdays and in San Marco on Saturdays. Mixing different types of linen or joining linen to other kinds of cloth was not allowed. Nor could any *linarolo* buy linen for resale only or cede it to anyone who was not a member of the guild. Shipowners and the *squeraroli* were exempted from this rule, but only insofar as the quantity requested fulfilled the needs of the ships.
Varoteri (furriers), *vagineri* (producers of haberdashery), *calegheri* (shoemakers), *orefici* (goldsmiths), *giupponieri* (tailors) and *coroneri* constituted a sector which occasionally had contacts that were anything but insignificant.
The first seat of the *varoteri* was at the Gesuiti, then, after 1725, in Campo Santa Margherita. Patron saints were the Virgin Mary, Saint Mary Elizabeth and St. Lazarus. In the 13th century they were divided into three *colonnelli* or families: lambskins, wild animals (*opera selvaggia*) and old skins (*opera vecchia*). Up until the 11th century fur trimming and linings were indispensable for gloves, hoods, caps and hats. In the 12th century furs also appeared in women's dress, even if the sumptuary laws tried to discourage every form of luxury. The patron saint of the *vagineri* was Saint Helen and as seat they had the church of San Geminiano. They made cases for needles, knives, fans, scissors, books, combs, perfume vials, pens and even inkpots, as well as for goblets for personal use, confectioneries. The cases were normally made of leather but in special cases might be in precious metals and wood. The leather was delivered in sheets to the *vagineri* by the *corporazione dei conzacurame*. The *calegheri* initially had their headquarters in the Calle delle Botteghe and then after 1446 in Campo San Toma. Their patron was Saint Ananias and the altar was in the church of San Toma. They had to use « new » leather while the *zavattieri* had to use only old leather for the clogs and slippers they made. The confraternity had to give the doganessa a pair of clogs each year of the value of 22 Venetian lire.
The *orefici* (goldsmiths) originally had their headquarters in the church of San Salvador and then care of the altar of the church of San Giovanni Elemosinario. Saint Anthony Abbot was their patron saint. The alloy was guaranteed and controlled by the *Messeri agli ori e agli argenti* in the Mint. From 1516 on the *tocadori* made the rounds of the various shops every week to control the gold and the silver and eliminate any kind of fraud. Hebrews were not admitted into the guilds; with a decree of 1331 it was established that goldwork could be sold only in the Rialto.
The *giupponieri* had their seat in Campo dei Gesuiti and at the altar of the church. They belonged to the tailors guild which was divided into three *colonnelli*: vestiary, *ziponi* and hose. The first would make clothing, skirts and furs (for men and women); the second worked on tunics, quilted clothing, bedclothes and the jackets which had to be made with old or new cloth but never with the two together. The patron saint of the

coroneri was Saint Francis and the headquarters of the guild were in Santa Trinita. They made wreaths, rosaries, buttons, using above all various types of wood. Some beads of wild boxwood or oxhorn were sent to Murano and covered with glass.
Medici (doctors) and *farmacisti* (pharmacists) had a much more ample field for their professions than they do nowadays, nor were their functions precisely defined. Many of the old tasks now assigned to the doctor were then attributed to the barber. The barbers'association was highly esteemed; its seat from 1468 on was in a building at Santa Maria dei Servi. The patron saints were Saints Damian and Cosma. Barbers were prohibited from shaving their customers on Sundays and on Christmas, unless they were ill; in this case the razor could not be used a second time.
The barber-doctor was permitted to perform venesection (phlebotomy) or bloodletting and apply bloodsuckers or cupping glasses, effectuate dental cures, remove corns, etc. In the 14th century he was allowed to keep his shop open at night as well; at the end of the 15th century a course in anatomy was required. The Health Authorities themselves turned to the barbers for help in the case of an epidemic and they were also called to serve on the ships of the Republic as doctors. The various *colonnelli* of the guild were: the *stueri*, whose shop-*stue* were rather like *calidaria* and where they offered their services for the cure and removal of corns but also provided hospitality to prostitutes; the *norsini*, who treated genital organs, hernias and removed gall stones; the *braglieri* who prepared hernia supports and castrated animals; the *conzaossi* for broken bones or sprains; the *levatrici* or midwives.

THE THIRTEENTH CENTURY

The chronicles of Daniele Barbaro inform us that in 1222 Doge Pietro Ziani proposed moving the capital to Constantinople and it would have been approved but for a single vote.
After the death of Enrico Dandolo the doge was flanked by a *consilium ducis* composed of a counselor for each of the six districts. This Lesser Council then limited still further the powers of the doge.
The power of Venice in the Mediterranean and its possessions were bound to irritate Genoa and thus the long bitter war for the possession of the trading ports of call in Syria began. In 1258 the Latin Empire disintegrated and the Greeks returned to Byzantium. Genoa at this point sided with Michael Palaeologus and in exchange received the same privileges enjoyed by the Venetians from 1204 on in addition to various islands such as Chios, Mitilene, Crete and Negroponte. Genoa was also given freedom of the seas in the Orient and the Black Sea. The city however at the same time was scheming with the king of Sicily to restore the Latin Empire of the East and when Michael Palaeologus got wind of this ambiguous attitude of the Genoese ex-allies he stipulated a pact with Venice which assured the latter the status quo.
Venice on the other hand also stipulated a truce with Genoa and the two cities accepted their respective zones of influence. But the Republic still found itself faced with other problems for it had to defend its trade in Istria, carry on the war with Ancona and settle the question of the uprisings in Crete. A treaty with Charles of Anjou ensured Venice support for the Latin reconquest of the Eastern Empire in exchange for the renewal of the privileges it had enjoyed prior to 1261. These projects however came to naught as a result of the « Sicilian Vespers » and new insurrections in Crete. Even the relations between Genoa and Venice, despite the truce, were once more deteriorating. Things were also further complicated throughout the area of Venetian possessions by the fact that the sultan of Egypt had conquered Acre, Beirut, Tyre and Sidon.
A memorable event in the history of the war between Genoa and Venice was the defeat of the Venetians at Curzola. The Republic however easily recovered the following year when, with a peace propitiated by Matteo Visconti, it obtained free access to navigation and trade in the Black Sea, as well as the safeguarding of her rights to maritime control.
In 1149, in the meanwhile, a *Consiglio dei Savi* (Assembly of Elders) had been constituted in addition to the Assembly and around 1172, as noted, a *Consilium Ducis*. The ducal councilors formed the *Minor Consiglio* (Lesser Council — executive), the Savi formed the *Maggior Consiglio* (Great Council). The Arengo therefore had only to ratify what had already been decided elsewhere.
In 1207 the *Maggior Consiglio* had 35 members elected by an electoral college of three members nominated in turns of three from the *Trentacie* in which the population was divided. Between 1207 and 1220 the *Quarantia* (Council of Forty — judiciary) was created and in 1255 the *Consiglio dei Rogati* (*Pregadi*) composed of sixty members. At a given time the members of the *Maggior Consiglio* rose to 1001, the electoral College was increased to four and later six members, subsequently divided into yearly and half-yearly electors. The latter elected the replacements for those who had moved on to other offices.
In 1286 the heads of the *Quarantia* proposed that the descendents of those who had already been part of the *Maggior Consiglio* should have the right to be elected. The proposal was rejected as was the one presented ten years later. The motion presented by Doge Pietro Gradenigo to admit those who had been members in the precedent quadriennium for a term of six months (that could be renewed) was accepted. The descendents of those who had been members up to 1172, moreover, could be elected by a college of three electors (always convalidated by the *Quarantia* according to the normal procedure). The results werethus a more extensive *Maggior Consiglio* (in 1340 the members were 1212).

THE FOURTEENTH CENTURY AND THE PLOT OF BAJAMONTE TIEPOLO

Venice, in the early 14th century, was shaken first by the unsuccessful conspiracy of Marin Bocconio and then by the dispute over Ferrara with Pope Clement V who had succeeded in getting all the traditional enemies of Venice to his side: the people of Padua, Lucca, Florence and Ancona. This war lay at the origins of the plot headed in 1310 by Bajamonte Tiepolo, a man who was very popular in Venice and related to the Querini of Ca' Grande and the Badoer. Taking advantage of the discomfort in the wake of the recent Venetian defeat at Castel Tedaldo and the interdict of the pope regarding commerce, the faction opposing the doge and under the leadership of the *Case Vecchie* of the nobles decided to overthrow the power of Gradenigo and invited Bajamonte Tipeolo to head the plot.
The uprising was to break out at dawn on June 15, 1310 but a thunderstorm threw the conspirators into confusion, preventing Badoero Badoer's group from arriving in time. They were in the Paduan countryside and were supposed to arrive to take the defenders of the doge from behind after the attack of the Querini and of Tiepolo. The doge, in the meantime, having learned of the plot from Marco Doner who had dissociated himself, had taken protective measures and requested reinforcements from the podestas of Chioggia, Murano and Torcello. When Marco Querini arrived at Ponte dei Dai with his men, he was met in the piazza by a group of armed men under the command of the Dandolo who killed

Ponte di Rialto, built in wood, as it looked at the end of the 15th cent. (Vittore Carpaccio, Cure of a Lunatic, detail).

him and put the others to flight. Bajamonte Tiepolo, for his part, arrived from the Mercerie at the alder which was in San Zulian and took his time, perhaps informed of what was happening in the square, dividing the armed men he commanded into two groups: one was to continue to the Spadiaria, the other was to branch off towards the Mercerie. Both groups were intercepted and had to deviate towards Rialto. Tiepolo took refuge on the far side of the Ponte della Moneta after having sawn it through and barricaded himself in the district which supported the *Case Vecchie*. The rout of Tiepolo's men was marked by the death of the standard bearer, hit on the head by a mortar that fell from a window of one of the houses when a certain Giustina Rossi, afterwards known as « *la vecia del morter* » (the old lady of the mortar) leaned out on her balcony in the Mercerie.
The common people in the meanwhile had stormed the office of the Magistrature of the police of the *Cinque alla Pace*, while the group under Marco Querini, who had been killed, had reorganized its files and renewed battle. They were however beaten at San Luca, and dispersed by a contingent of brothers of the Scuola Grande della Carta and the members of the painters' guild.
Badoero Badoer, arrested by the podestà in Chioggia, was taken to Venice and beheaded. Bajamonte however, in exchange for surrender, succeeded in obtaining permission to go into exile together with the conspirator members of the *Maggior Consiglio*, prohibited from stopping in Padua, Treviso, Vicenza and the cities at war with Venice.
Giustina Rossi's request that her rent not be increased was granted and she was allowed to display a commemorative standard at the window every year. In fact up until 1797 on the day of San Vito a standard with the Lion of Saint Mark was exhibited in the house of the « *vecia del morter* ». The last one is now in the Museo Correr.
A new attempt by Bajamonte Tiepolo to get the people to rise up was crushed. The warrant for his arrest emitted by the Senate however was never served, for all news of Tiepolo's whereabouts came to an end in 1329.
Once the story with Bajamonte Tiepolo had been taken care of, the city began to consider her role and relationship with other nations and other cities. Venice became aware of the ever-increasing difficulty in maintaining a monopoly on trade with the East and set about directing her interests to the north as well, to Vienna and Nürnberg, Leipzig and Lübeck. Genoa, for her part, after defeating the Maroccan blockade of Gibralter had opened the routes on the Atlantic and had reached the great markets of Bruges, abbreviating the land routes.
Costs diminished via sea and Venice soon captured most of the trade with Flanders and England. Progress had also been made in naval techniques with the introduction of the compass and rudder, so that now much larger galleys could be built with a crew of two hundred sailors, if need be ready to defend the shipload from the pirates. Trade with China had also opened up and caravans of Christians began to travel the silk route through Europe, Persia and China. In 1326 there already seem to have been Franciscan friars, in charge of an inn for foreigners, in the Chinese city of Zayton. In 1345 Venice had to deal with still one more rebellion in Zara, instigated by Louis of Anjou, and succeeded in putting it down. In 1347 the city was struck by an earthquake, a sea-quake and the plague, which reaped hundreds of thousands of victims throughout Europe.
The first half of the 14th century saw Venice seriously involved on the Mainland. With Cangrande, the Della Scala had extended their dominions up to Vicenza, Belluno, Feltre and Padua; in 1329 they also took Treviso and Venice found herself in danger of a blockade of supplies via the mainland. Upon his death, right after the taking of Treviso, Cangrande was succeeded by his nephews Alberto and Mastino II and a sort of customs protectionism towards the goods coming from Venice immediately began. There was also a marked withdrawal of foodstuffs on their way to Venice and the economy was seriously jeopardized. Venice answered by raising her own customs taxes on merchandise from the East headed to Verona, but with only slight effects, for they were almost all luxury goods. Finally, despite her general reluctance to fighting on the mainland, Venice decided to ally herself with Florence, which had been deprived of Lucca and Parma by the Scaligeri, driving out the Rossi. And it was one of the Rossi, Pietro, who was set at the head of the troops which had convened against the Scaligeri in 1336, troops which also included French and German contingents.
After the first victories, the Gonzaga and the Estensi of Ferrara also joined the alliance and, surrounded, Mastino sued for peace via Marsilio da Carrara, who had been left in Padua as a representant after he had been deprived of the signoria of the city. During his conversations with the doge, Marsilio offered Venice Padua in exchange for being put in charge. The Scaligeri were defeated and forced to sign the peace in 1339 and Venice ended up with Padua, under the management of the Carrara, and Treviso and the eastern Mark as far as Sacile to govern by herself. Venice now had a frontier to defend and a hinterland to organize: in Treviso, as afterwards in all the other cities on the mainland, the organization of the lagoon was reproduced to scale. Power was entrusted to a podestà, controlled by a rector, who was also Venetian, and was in charge of the police and responsible for all the acts of government to the doge and the Senate, a fairly large city council which concerned itself with taxes, streets and communication routes and the social life of the city.
In 1340 Venice once more turned its attentions to the East in answer to the appeal of Byzantium when the Ottoman Turks installed themselves less than fifty miles from the capital. In the 1340s the construction of the granary on the Molo and the convent of the Servi was also begun, both torn down in the early 19th century. Work also began on the Doges' Palace which was to terminate with the building in its present form in the first quarter of the 15th century. Operations in the East against the Turks and the consequent idyll with Genoa continued until the Black Death of 1347-48, which arrived in Italy on the ships of the two Republics. In Venice it reaped up to 600 lives a day and at the end a city which had had a population of almost 200,000, had lost almost 120,000. The tension with Genoa, which had already degenerated into skirmishes before the plague, broke out anew in 1350 and continued for three years with alternating vicissitudes which bled both cities white. On August 19, 1353, Venetian ships arrived in Sardinia under the command of Nicolò Pisani, in aid of the allied Aragonese fleet which was besieging Alghero, achieved a

splendid victory in the battle of Lojera against the ships of Antonio Grimaldi, avenging the grave defeat of the year before in Galata. Genoa, brought to her knees by the fact that both trade and food supplies were blocked by the closing of the Tyrrhenian sea, surrendered to Giovanni Visconti, archbishop and lord of Milan, the neighbor Venice had created with her new possessions on the Mainland. The naval war in any case continued. Visconti however preferred to send Francesco Petrarch to Venice to negotiate peace, which Venice refused to discuss. The naval war continued with incursions on both sides until Nicolò Pisani's Venetian fleet was attacked by Paganino Doria in the bay of Portolengo in the Peloponnesus and destroyed in 1354.
In the meanwhile Marin Falier was elected new doge. He had been ambassador at the pope's court in Avignon and had a good diplomatic career behind him.
Falier was faced with great tension in Venice as a result of the economic crisis which had practically exhausted the city's finances. It is not easy to guess what the reasons were that persuaded the old doge to try and overthrow the Republic and become prince. In addition to reacting to the malicious rumors spread by the nobility, there is also the historically more plausible hypothesis of a maneuver by the new merchant class which was excluded from the government and which aspired to the political and economic domination of the city. Whatever the case may be, the conspiracy organized by the doge, who depended on the *Arsenalotti*, his traditional body guard, failed because someone warned the *Maggior Consiglio*. The *Dieci* rapidly organized the trial, convoked the highest magistrates and condemned the conspirators to be hanged at the windows of the Doges' Palace. Marin Falier, who made a full confession, was beheaded on April 18, 1355 at sunset, on the very spot on the staircase of the Palace courtyard where, when he was elected, he had pronounced his *promissione* or vow of observance and fidelity to the laws.
His successor Giovanni Gradenigo signed the peace treaty with Genoa, permitting Venice to turn her thoughts with greater tranquility to the problems arising on the Mainland, where the Hungarian king was advancing. A diplomatic agreement, whereby Venice relinquished Dalmatia, settled the question of the Hungarians who had already arrived at Mestre. Tensions in Candia however were once more coming to a head, with Venetian nobles in ferment and asking for reduced taxes, supported by the Greek population. The rebellion was put down by troops under the command of Luchin dal Verme, from Verona, and on June 4, 1364, Petrarch was able to see from the house he lived in on the Riva degli Schiavoni the galleys of the conquerors returning to the port of Venice with their masts decorated with laurel. In the meanwhile Genoa had succeeded in bringing all the traditional enemies of Venice to her side: Padua, the Austrian duchy, the king of Hungary. Venice managed to make allies of the king of Cyprus and the Visconti of Milan, to whom all the conquests on the Mainland were promised, while Venice was to keep those on the seas. The clash saw the hostilities off to a start with the Genovese in the lead. After having been defeated at Anzio, they surprised Vettor Pisani's Venetian fleet wintering in Pola and destroyed it. The other fleet under the leadership of Carlo Zen was in the East, and as a result the Genovese arrived as far as Chioggia after wreaking havoc in Grado, Caorle, and Pellestrina, directly threating the Lido, while Francesco da Carrara closed in by land. Pisani, re-elected *capitano da mar*, was furnished with forty ships fitted out in record time with which he managed to block Chioggia for a year, completely cutting off communications, for the inland water-ways were also closed by sinking hulls in them. On January 1, 1380, Carlo Zen's fleet returned from the Orient; this intervention turned the scales in favor of the Venetian forces who the following June succeeded in beating the Genovese, capturing nineteen galleys and 4,500 men. With the peace of Turin the following year, Venice, while confirming anew the cession of Dalmatia to the king of Hungary, was now faced with a rival that had been prostrated and was lacerated by internal conflicts, leaving the way free in the East where the Republic enlarged her trade bases, acquiring Corfu, Nauplia, Argo, Scutari, Durazzo. Absolute mistress of the seas and of trade, Venice could now turn her attention to new enterprises in the Mainland.
The eye of Venice fell first of all on the Duchy of Milan and when in 1402 the state of affairs in northern Italy became confused and difficult as a result of the death of Galeazzo Visconti, Venice did not hesitate to take advantage of the situation and occupy Feltre, Padua and Verona. The same administrative system already tested in Treviso was set up with « rectors » (podestà or captains) elected by the *Maggior Consiglio* from among its members.

Doge Agostino Barbarigo on his way to receive Caterina Cornaro, Queen of Cyprus, on June 1, 1489.

THE FIFTEENTH CENTURY

In less than fifty years Venice had succeeded in opening the seaways with the defeat of Genoa, and the trade routes to the North with the formation of farflung, rich and prosperous possessions which were waiting to be conveniently exploited. No longer hampered by duty and the like, wood from the mountains of Belluno, grain and wine from the plains, thriving industries of wool, linen, paper, all meant profits which arrived in Venice making her self-sufficient and increasing her wealth. Dominion meant this, as well as prestige.
At the beginning of the 15th century Venice already had an active fleet of over 3,500 units, an Arsenal with 16,000 specialized laborers, markets ranging from the Far East to Flanders and England in which she dealt in spices, sugar, luxurious garments, wool and silk, Malvasia — the Greek wine which together with salt was a monopoly, and slaves. The state regulated naval activity, from ownership of the ships to trade contracts, the routes, the dates of departure and arrival of the convoys, the management of the maritime ports of call. It regulated labor, forbidding the departure of technology from Venice (specialized workers could not leave the city) while it attracted skilled labor from abroad. It created a state system of medical assistence with refresher and training courses for physicians, and a body of twelve worked exclusively for the State which provided their wages. Even after the Hebrews, who had practically a financial monopoly of the city, were sent away and then readmitted with strict limitations, Jewish doctors were invited to stay. Venice protected the foreigners and special officials kept an eye out for fraud or abuses which might bring them harm, setting herself up as a city in which to sojourn, a city from which to leave easily and safely for all

destinations. The 15th century opened onto a brilliant future, still however accompanied by the after-effects of the problems that had presented themselves in the second half of the 14th century. While it is true that Venice managed to avoid taking sides in the schism of the West, despite the fact that one of the two popes deposed by the council of Pisa, Clement, was a Venetian, and while she succeeded in buying Dalmatia for 100,000 florins from Ladislas of Naples who had had himself elected king of Hungary, his successor Sigismund reacted vehemently and sent a large army commanded by Pippo Spano into the Veneto from Friuli. For two years this army ceaselessly laid waste to the hinterland and in 1412 even attempted a landing on the Lido, to be beaten only a few months later at Motta di Livenza by a river fleet.

A truce with Sigismund was declared in 1413, but the war was not to be concluded until years later, during the determining encounter with the Visconti.

In the meanwhile in the East the Turks, with whom Venice had made another pact in 1413, with the future doge Francesco Foscari in charge of negotiations, had encircled the Byzantine empire which was reduced to all effects to the capital alone. Three years after the pact, in 1416, a Turkish fleet attacked Negroponte, a Venetian colony, and the sea captain Pietro Loredan was forced to stand battle at Gallipoli, where he won. As a result, for a certain period of time it was thought that Venice by herself would be able to halt the Turks. In 1418 Sigismund once more invaded Friuli while Venice had continued her diplomatic activity allying herself with Naples. Sigismund was supported by the patriarchate of Aquileia and the counts of Gorizia, but her knowledge of the territory came to the aid of Venice as well as the ability of Tristano Sorvognan, a noble Udinese. Under his command, the patriarch was forced to remain in Udine where he was besieged in 1420. Sigismund was forced to withdraw on account of problems connected with his inheritance of the kingdom of Bohemia in 1419, and Udine surrendered. All of Friuli became Venetian with the exception of Aquileia, San Daniele and San Vito; the Serenissima now stretched all the way to the Alps, a natural line of defense. To the west there was still the problem of Filippo Maria Visconti, who had risen to power in 1412. For several years around 1421, after its conquest of Genoa, Florence attempted to draw Venice into an anti-Visconti league but was unsuccessful. Venice did not act until 1425, with the arrival of Carmagnola, one of the century's most famous mercenaries, a former captain of Visconti and ex-governor in his name of Genoa. The information he volunteered and his offer to enter into the services of the Republic, together with the concrete peril of the formation of a unitary state in the center-north which would certainly have invaded the vulnerable plain up to the lagoons, induced the city to enter in league with Florence in 1426 and to accept the services of Carmagnola at a price that for the times was extraordinarily high. The relations with the « Mainland captain » however became ever less satisfactory: it was a never-ending procrastination and hiking up the price, while Carmagnola kept up relations with Milan of which he informed the Senate. Venice accepted the surrender of Brescia, which had for some time tended to side with Venice, then captured and lost a series of river bases along the Po in the Cremonese, and finally almost had to force Carmagnola to enter action. The captain's greatest victory was in 1427 at Maclodio where he captured (and immediately released!) the entire Visconti army. In 1428 peace was signed in which Venice extended her boundaries up to the river Adda. In 1431 war was renewed and Carmagnola became so suspect that after the loss of a fleet at Soncino, Venice formally recalled him.

In 1432 the captain made no move against Cremona and lost four cities. At this point the patience of Venice had reached the breaking point: Carmagnola was recalled and arrested, and executed in May. In 1437 Venice obtained the acknowledgement and the investiture of all her territories from the Friuli to the river Adda from Sigismund who was irritated with Milan. This justified her legally as well in the face of claims. Venice then hired Gattamelata as Captain and initiated a series of encounters in an attempt to liberate Brescia which was being besieged by Filippo Maria Visconti, a terrible siege that did not end until 1440 and which demonstrated how strong the feeling against Milan was in the city. In 1441 Venice inherited Ravenna; in 1446, her troops under the command of Francesco Sforza beat Milan at Casalmaggiore and arrived almost up to the base of the city walls. Foreign threats, soon to bring the French and the Spanish to Italy, began to hover over Milan. It was not until 1454 that Lodi witnessed the signing of the peace and the creation of the Holy League which aimed at guaranteeing peace and the *status quo* between the principal unified Italian states: Venice, Milan, Florence and the Papal States. In 1453 however Constantinople had fallen under the attack of the Turks of Mohammed II the Conqueror. By 1416 the Turkish power had pushed as far as Eubea and the Cyclades, in 1430 it also occupied Thessalonica and forced Venice to reduce its privileges to the right of trade only. Refugees from what had once been the Empire of the East flowed into Venice — the most Byzantine city of the West. This flow had already begun with the first Turkish invasion. The « crusade » of Pius II and the Doge Moro in 1464 failed before it even started. An alliance was made with Hungary which, however, was unable to resist the Turks for long; in 1469 Venice learned that the objective of Mohammed II was at this point Eubea, Negroponte, the largest of the Greek islands and her major commercial base still in operation. Despite the fact that Venice, by imposing new taxes, reducing the wages of her officials, rounding up what money she could on the Mainland, had enlarged the Arsenal and launched a rather imposing fleet, Negroponte, already besieged by Mohammed II, fell through an obvious error of the sea captain Nicolò Canal who, after having manoeuvred against the bridge of Turkish boats which ensured their contacts with the mainland, turned back. Canal was exiled and Venice found herself in a position where she could do little else but harass the Turks who were, so to say, right on her doorstep. Twice Turkish raids arrived as far as the river Livenza in Friuli and thus in 1479 Venice was forced to sign a peace treaty which left her only Durazzo in the Balkans and levied a heavy tribute on her for trading in the Black Sea. In 1481 the situation improved slighly when Mohammed II died and Venice was able to rent Zante from his successor Bajazet II. One of the political consequences of the peace of 1479 was that Venice was discredited making it possible, on the occasion of the war with Ercole d'Este in 1481, for Milan, Florence and Naples, and subsequently the Church, to take sides against Venice which was also struck by a new interdict in 1483. Venice refused to receive this interdict materially, while the letter with which the Senate communicated that it would appeal to a Council against Sixtus IV was delivered to Rome by nailing it to the door of a church. The war ended the following year with a treaty by which Polesine and Rovigo passed to the Republic. The only acquisition of this period for Venice was that of Cyprus through Caterina Cornaro, in 1489. Caterina, daughter of Marco Corner, had gone as bride in 1472 to Giacomo II di Lusignano, but when they were officially engaged the Senate had had the bride sign a donation « in case he should die without a legitimate heir ». When Giacomo died leaving Caterina pregnant, a fleet was sent to protect the island and after the failure of a plot, Caterina was flanked by two Venetian advisors. At the end, caught between the pressures exerted by Venice and the intrigues of her court, she gave in and abdicated in favor of the Republic. Received in Venice by the Doge Barbarigo and all the highest authorities Caterina renewed her act of donation in San Marco. In exchange for Cyprus she received an annual pension of 8,000 gold ducats, continued to be called « Queen » and in her estate of Asolo held court, attended by the most important humanists of her time.

THE SIXTEENTH CENTURY

Charles VIII, king of France and cousin of the future Louis XII, the duke of Orleans, who claimed his rights to the Duchy of Milan where Ludovico il Moro, had come into power, descended into Italy in 1494. When Charles took Naples in 1495 and even Lodovico il Moro, who had invited him to Italy in the hopes of using him against Florence and the Church, realized that Louis of Orleans' pretensions to the duchy were not words but facts, as shown by the taking of Novara, Venice sought contacts with Spain, Milan, Austria, where Maximilian I of Hapsburg had been elected emperor, and the Papacy. The league sent out into the field an army of mercenaries, financed mostly by Venice, and attacked Charles VIII who was returning to France at Fornovo. It was a slaughter, passed off as a victory, and Charles passed through demonstrating that the entire peninsula was open for any unified state that wanted it. In 1449 at Blois Venice allied herself with Charles' successor, Louis XII, who had intentions of taking the Duchy of Milan. This was not in the least surprising if one considers the division that reigned among those who had been the members of the Holy League after the peace of Lodi, as well as the offers of enlarging her dominion which Venice obtained with the treaty of Blois. As was foreseeable, Milan quickly fell and Venice obtained Cremona.
But in the same year of 1449 a disaster took place in the East. Antonio Grimani, sea captain, lost the fleet and the colony of Lepanto. New Turkish raids reached from Friuli to Vicenza In the Peloponnesus Modone and Corone, « the eyes of th Serenissima », fell into Ottoman hands.
Since Venice was no longer capable of financing the war, i 1503 she signed a peace treaty with the Turks that sanctione the *status quo*. The economic blow had in fact come from th seas, from Columbus and above all from Vasco de Gama's si ships which were the first to sail from Portugal to the Indies It was no longer necessary to load wares from Asia in th Mediterranean; the English and German markets were n longer a prerogative of Venice; in Lisbon Florentine merchants achieved a privileged position while Venice was undecided whether or not to accept the offer of the Portugues king to go and load their wares there. The largest banks failed panic spread in Rialto (it was even planned to dig a canal between the Red Sea and the Mediterranean and the project wa rejected because of inadequate technical means), the tension were transformed into armed clashes in the streets.
With its traditional sources of wealth threatened, Venic turned her attentions to the Mainland and enlarging he dominions there. But her policy of gradually incorporating th pontificial cities in Romagna, offering asylum to their lord who had been ousted by Valentino, son of the Borgia pop Alexander VI, antagonized the new pope Julian II wh hastened to enter negotiations with all the European powers An initial alliance was signed in Blois with France and Maximilian I, but there was no follow up until a diplomatic incident provided the emperor with the chance to invade Venic as far as Vicenza in 1508, where he was blocked by the Veneti

Venice, Queen of the Seas (copy after an original by G. B. Tiepolo).

n troops under the command of Bartolomeo d'Alviano and Jiccolò di Pitigliano. To the contrary, with a counter-attack 'enice took over Istria and Gorizia. The diplomatic activity f the pope became frenetic and just how Venice and her ominions were to be divided up among the allies was decided. 'erona, Vicenza, Padua, Treviso and everything beyond the iver Mincio to Austria; Spain would get the possessions in 'uglia; Dalmatia went to Hungary; the Lombard cities to 'rance; and Rimini, Faenza and Cervia, the object of the riginal dispute, to the pope. The alliance was presented as a rusade and the treaty was signed in 1508, with the pope joinng up at the beginning of the following year. Venice found erself alone against the greatest powers of Europe, excomnunicated and interdicted. In April the French were in the)ominion and a few days later crossed the river Adda. Barolomeo d'Alviano, during a march, was intercepted at Agadello and had to stand battle. It was a disaster; Alviano was aken prisoner; there were any number of dead; the mercenares of Pitigliano — who had not participated in the battle — led. The Venetian policy which had turned to the Mainland once the sea was precluded, either because of the Turks or beause of the Atlantic sea routes, seemed to have been desroyed once and for all.
The city began preparing for a siege and the government took diplomatic steps in all directions in an attempt to detach her nemies from the league. The cities on the Mainland were eleased from their vows, but some of them remained loyal, uch as Treviso and Udine; elsewhere ties with Venice showed hemselves to be particularly tenacious among the working lasses and peasants. It was thanks above all to them that 'adua was reconquered a month and a half after its loss and he dillydallying and indecision of Maximilian made it possiole for them to hold out against the subsequent imperial siege. At the end of the year 1509 Vicenza too had been retaken, as vell as Belluno and its territory and the Euganean cities, while an attempt to assault Verona had failed.
But the grave problem of how to keep and defend these terriories remained to be solved and after futile attempts with the ultan and Henry VIII of England, Venice had to accept the humiliating conditions of peace imposed by Julius II. The reaty was concluded in 1510; at this point it also became clear hat the pope was changing his policy and was turning against is former ally, France. In 1511 however the papal army was defeated by the French captain Trivulzio at Mirandola and the pope's diplomatic activity even more doggedly aimed at isolatng the French. The Holy League was created at the end of the year. While the French had their hands full in Emilia, Brescia and Bergamo rebelled and once more turned to Venice. Shorty thereafter Brescia was taken by assault and sacked and plundered while Bergamo paid out 60,000 ducats to avoid the same fate.
Venice now found herself face to face with the problem of the territories occupied by Maximilian, who had no intention of ceding the Veneto, despite the fact that he had sent no more troops to either of the ex-companions of the league. In the meanwhile Louis XII had sent ambassadors to Venice asking for an alliance and, disappointed by the attitudes of her partners in the Holy League, accepted. In 1513 a new treaty was signed at Blois with France and Venice as allies. Shortly before, Julius II had died and Leo X, son of Lorenzo de' Medici, was elected in his place.
Even so, the war continued for various years, up until 1518 when Maximilian signed a truce with the city; in 1519 he died and the empire passed to his grandson Charles I of Spain, who became Charles V, and the war turned into a conflict between France and the Empire, while occasional crises — such as that of 1521 — were opened with Venice. The peace treaty with the Empire was signed in 1523 at Worms and all the territories in her possession were acknowledged. In 1525 she was among the signers of the league of Cognac with which the papacy supported the French, but in 1529 France was no longer up to continuing the war and the Peace of Cambrai, known as the « *paix des dames* », defined relationships with Charles V. Venice definitively ceded her possessions in Puglia to Spain; in 1530 the peace was perfected with the consecration of Charles V as emperor, which took place in Bologna. The problem — and not for Venice alone — was now once more that of the Turks.

Battista Agnolo del Moro: Soldiers of the Venetian Troops being Paid.

In 1535 François I signed a pact of alliance with Suleiman the Magnificent in which the Turks were to support the French attack in Flanders with an attack in Hungary and by sea. Venice was invited by Suleiman to participate in the alliance, breaking the one she had with the empire, in an obvious attempt at putting the Republic in a difficult plight. Venice refused and her trade with the East was blocked: in 1537 the Turks attacked Corfu which was saved by chance. The allies had not responded to Venice's request for aid. In 1538 Venice, the pope, and the empire launched a fleet that was however destroyed by the Turks at Prevesa in Epirus on account of the incorrect behavior of the Spanish under the command of Andrea Doria. Nauplia and Monemvasia fell in 1540 and that same year Venice had to sign a peace with Suleiman in which her trade rights were even further restricted: her dominion in the Mediterranean was slowly crumbling and she found herself in such economic straits that projects for new taxes were initiated. The reason why they never became effective was the unheard of confusion and incapacity of the Senate to agree on a line of government. Yet curiously enough this was balanced by one of the most felicitous periods from the point of view of art, town-planning and public expenditure in the city. Building of the patrician palaces on the Grand Canal continued, the layout of the Piazza was completed with the work of Sansovino, the Palladian masterpieces of the Churches of the Redentore and of San Giorgio Maggiore were built.
Trade in wool products greatly increased, artisans were creating objects of art that were in demand everywhere, and the embroidery and goldwork of Venice was becoming famous throughout the world. The general prosperity of the city, however, did not include everyone, for there were so many poor that the laws on public assistence were insufficient. Then there were also the prisoners, and for them the Prigioni Nuove at Ponte della Paglia were built, and then there were the slaves.
In addition there were vagabonds, professional gamblers and beggars for some of whom the Provveditori alla Sanità (health officials) granted actual « begging licenses ».
Moreover, in line with her traditions, the city also welcomed the Protestants (in the rest of Europe heretics were being

Doge Marino Grimani receiving gifts from the Persian ambassador.

burned at the stake) and refused to admit the right of the pope to judge them on Venetian territory — even though at the end of the century, after the Council of Trent, the Serenissima consigned Giordano Bruno to the pope. He had sought refuge with the Mocenigo and was here betrayed, arrested, tried, turned over to the papal representative and burned at the stake in the year 1600 in the Campo de' Fiori in Rome.
The Turks in the meanwhile were driving the Knights Hospitallers of St. John from Rhodes and in 1565 they unsuccessfully also attacked them in their new headquarters of Malta. In 1568 news of the Turkish intentions on Cyprus began to circulate. In 1570 the grand vizier of Constantinople delivered an ultimatum to the *bailo* according to which Venice was to cede the island. Shortly thereafter a Turkish ambassador took the ultimatum to the Senate. The Republic replied that Cyprus was hers and sought allies to get together a fleet, finding them in the pope and in Spain who set still another Genovese in command of the ships, Gian Andrea Doria. Things went badly from the start: there were delays and above all there was friction between Venice and Doria. The Turks invaded Cyprus before the fleet arrived and the ships had to turn back. Resistance on the island was entrusted to the population and the Venetian garrison. Besieged in Famagosta, the latter surrendered on terms but were nevertheless barbarously massacred by the enemy. The Venetians had to wait until October of 1571 for revenge. After the principles of Christianity had finally been agreed on, a fleet arrived near Lepanto where the Turkish fleet composed of 230 galleys, 70 smaller ships, 90,000 men and 750 pieces of artillery under the command of Ali Pascia was to be found. After an extenuating battle in which the Spanish and Venetian fleet got the better of the Turks, while Doria behaved exactly as he had the year before creating confusion, the victory of the Christian ships was achieved, although at high cost with 7,500 dead (including 4,500 Venetians) and 20,000 wounded. In Venice the Turkish merchants were forced to barricade themselves in their Fondaco to escape the crowd and there was great jubilation over the victory. It was however quite impossible for Venice to continue a war with the Turks and it was clear that Spain and the pope had no intentions of helping her, so that in 1573 a new pact was signed which, to all effects, corroborated the end of the great maritime empire Venice had created in the centuries past.
Once relations with the East had been settled, although not as Venice had hoped for, ties with Spain gradually weakened as a result of the Turkish question and the Serenissima drew closer to France. The visit of Henry III in 1574, on his way home from Poland to receive the crown after the death of the king, his brother Charles IX, was the occasion both to show Venetian hospitality and wealth to a great power, as well as that of reconfirming friendly relations with France. Two years later the city was struck by the plague and even had to turn some of its ships into floating hospitals. Fifty thousand people died, the city voted to build the church of the Redentore as thanks for the end of the epidemic, entrusting the project to Palladio. Another building which has become a symbol of the city, the Doges' Palace, was rebuilt in those years after two terrifying fires, and despite the fact that plans for a radical transformation were proposed, the city decided to restore it as it was.
In 1579 the ties between Venice and Florence were consolidated thanks to a woman, Bianca Cappello, first mistress and then second wife of Francesco I de' Medici, to whose wedding a delegation of representatives was invited.

THE SEVENTEENTH AND EIGHTEENTH CENTURIES

The end of the 16th century as well as the beginnings of the 17th were characterized by the dramatic crisis which had opened between the city and the Council of Ten, whose fields of competence had grown in its century and a half of life to the point where it was no longer possible to discern whether the areas in which the Ten acted were legitimately theirs or to what extent they were valid. The council had approved permanent *zonte* (juntas) as early as 1529 and had nominated subcommittees with executive powers in 1539 with three *Inquisitori di stato* and in 1537 with the *Esecutori contro la bestemmia*, a sort of « vice squad ».
It was an act of the Ten which in 1605 brought the crisis with the Church to a head and led to the fulmination of the interdict, the last in the history of the papacy, which forbade the Venetian clergy from exercising their functions. Some priests were accused of acts of indecency and violence. After the sentence, the pope maintained that only Rome could judge the priests and sent the interdict in a parcel which arrived just after the death of the doge. The next doge, Leonardo Donà, opened it a month later. It was a legal war and Venice entrusted the defenses to the friar Paolo Sarpi, the historian of the Council of Trent.
Sarpi was extremely able and the government refused to accept the interdict, ordering the clergy to continue as before. Public opinion in all of Europe, except Spain, sided with Venice and Paul V made a fool of himself, until Venice made up her mind to accept French mediation and the interdict was revoked.
The crisis with the church was solved, but two others immediately came to a head with foreign powers: in 1617 the Friuli war broke out with Austria because Venice sent an expedition of her own to put down the attacks of the Uscocchi, since Ferdinand of Austria seemed to be doing nothing. The second crisis was of a diplomatic nature due to the discovery of a conspiracy — rather in the style of an operetta — to overthrow the government, led by the viceroy of Naples and the Spanish ambassador, and implicating any number of others. Their intentions moreover were to capture the nobles, get ransom and create a principality for the viceroy in the Adriatic. As was to be expected the Ten acted rapidly, threw the *bravi* (mercenaries who hired themselves out as bodyguards above all to foreigners) out of the city, strangled and hung head downwards three of them in the Piazzetta, condemning more discreetly about 300 others to death. Another more tragic act of the Ten involved the senator, Antonio Foscarini, accused of espionage for the English, executed in 1621 and restored to

honor the following year (as can be read in the slab then placed on his tomb in S. Stae).
Venice was involved in another local war, centered around the Valtellina, in 1523. The valley had been occupied by the Spanish so as to establish a bridge between Milan and Austria and in 1623 an alliance was formed with Richelieu and the Savoia. But while in 1624 the French had liberated the Valtellina by driving out the papal troops, in 1626 in agreement with Spain they constituted it into a free state and Venice had to accept. The plague that broke out in 1630 reaped almost 50,000 victims and Venice was faced, on the one hand, by this scourge and, on the other, had to keep her eyes on events in Crete (Candia for the Venetians) where there had been a rupture in relations with the Sultan Ibrahim who accused the Venetians of favoring the « Corsican war » of the Knights of Malta. The war of Candia, in any case, continued for twenty-four years (twenty-two of which under siege), since the allies (Rome, Tuscany, Naples and Malta), assailed by doubts and disagreements, preferred to steer clear of a frontal encounter with the Turkish fleet. It was to finance the war in Candia that the proposal to reopen the Maggior Consiglio was presented, to all extents and purposes selling membership to citizens who offered to maintain a thousand soldiers for a year and who would underwrite a promise for 60,000 ducats. The proposal made by the Senate was rejected by the Maggior Consiglio, but passed when the ducats to be paid rose to 100,000. It was all however to no avail for Candia was lost to Venice when Francesco Morosini was forced to sign the peace treaty with the Turks although the Serenissima preserved her naval bases of Suda, Gabrusa and Spinalonga.
On September 26th, the « sea captain » Morosini left Candia after 465 years of dominion, carrying almost the entire population off to Venice, with the relics, the images and ecclesiastical vessels, as well as the archives, and was brought to trial for having surrendered.
It was however obvious that he could not have done otherwise and he was acquitted and continued to direct the war for the Morea. In 1683 Vienna was besieged by the Turks and asked for help. Initially the Republic refused to commit herself on land but adhered to the request the following year when the war shifted to sea. As allies she had the emperor, the pope and the king of Poland. On this occasion Modone, Nauplia, Patrasso, Corinth and Lepanto were retaken. It was during this campaign in 1687 that a shell launched by the cannons of the « Königsmark » hit the Parthenon in which the Turks had installed a powder house and destroyed the finest monument of the Athens of Pericles. With the peace of Karlowitz of January 26, 1699, Venice retained the Morea, Aegina, Santa Maura, Zante and some of her conquests in Dalmatia and in Albania.
With the death of Charles II of Spain on November 1, 1700, large clouds began to gather on the horizons in Europe on account of the succession claimed both by Louis XIV of France and Leopold, emperor of Austria. Venice found herself being courted by both aspirants, but after weighing the advantages and dangers of siding with one or the other, the Senate opted for an armed neutrality which was not however always respected by the contenders, while the hinterland which Venice could not defend was devastated as the armies continuously passed through. The role of mediator between the two powers for the treaty of Utrecht in 1713 went to Venice. In the meanwhile in 1714 the *bailo* of Constantinople was informed that the Turks intended to declare war and by the following year the Turks had already taken back Morea; in 1716 they besieged Corfù and forced Venice to make an alliance with the empire. The siege on Corfù was lifted and in 1717 the fleet commanded by Ludovico Flangini destroyed the Turkish fleet. Even though the war seemed to be going in her favor, Venice, under threat of a separate peace, was forced by Austria to sign the peace treaty of Passarowitz in 1718 in which she retained her most recent conquests in the Epirus but had to cede the Morea and the other Aegean and Cretan bases to the Turks. In the years that followed Venice licked her wounds but also dedicated most of her financial resources to public works. The first thing she did was to increase the defenses of the territory of the lagoon by constructing the *murazzi*, a large breakwater dam which reaches from Malamocco to Chioggia, to protect the shores from the violence of the tides and which has stood up fairly well up to now. The ruling classes however were in crisis: the patricians were worn out by internal struggles among the forty families who held the power and were growing richer and richer and the « *barnabotti* » (so-called from the district of San Barnaba where most of them lived), the fallen nobility who survived on subsistence and who were also more open to the new ideas arriving from Europe. All commercial and industrial activity at this point had passed into the hands of the bourgeoisie. The city was rich and attracted tourists and persons of culture, but an analysis of its wealth reveals the profound changes that had taken place since she had lost her maritime empire. Trade was no longer in oriental goods which had almost become a monopoly of the Dutch East India Company but was centered on locally produced wares (oil, wine, salt, products of the Greek islands which were still in the possession of Venice) which were marketed in the Mediterranean and the interior thanks to the reactivation of river shipping. The Venetian fleet, the most modern and the best in the 16th century, had been superceded by the Dutch and English fleets: Venice had very few modern sailing ships with cannons below deck, and continued to build and use galleys with oars, undoubtedly easier to maneuver in waters like the Mediterranean, but costly and with a limited autonomy, and unable to defend themselves from pirate attacks unless they were still travelling in convoys and therefore at a slower speed. It was not until the middle of the 18th century that permission was given for ships with more than twenty-four cannons and with a crew of more than forty men to set sail by themselves, with the result that these became the ships most in demand and the Arsenal built its share. The port of Venice was also supplanted by that of Trieste, declared an open port by the emperor, and by Ancona, while the Venetian patrols were no longer capable of exacting their traditional toll from the faster ships as they entered the Adriatic. By this time the nobility considered commerce an activity that was not in keeping with their rank and invested in the Mainland. Venice enriched its treasury in 1776 by confiscating goods on the Mainland with the suppression of 127 pieces of church property, a confiscation which brought in about three million ducats.
In the international field things went even worse: the decline was by now evident and diplomacy itself had a hard time making itself credible. The fact that Venice constantly pursued a policy of neutrality in the Polish and Austrian wars of succession, as previously mentioned, meant that the Republic was absent both at the peace table in Vienna and at that which guaranteed the throne to Maria Teresa. Venice, in other words, not only gained nothing, but ended up by having to submit to the requisitions of the Austrian troops and the havoc they wreaked in her territories, some of which Austria had all intentions of annexing.
Included among these territories were Dalmatia, the Valsugana, Friuli. In addition, these possessions were defended by men not always capable of living up to their task. The « *sradioti* » Venice hired in Albania and in Dalmatia were few. There was a light cavalry which was not always trustworthy because it was poorly armed, and then there were the « *cernide* » composed of three thousand men. Giovanni Morosini wrote at the time that the « *cernide* were composed of the most wretched people in the land, so poor they could not live without their pay for two days, not trained in the use of arms, undisciplined and so unused to military service that they had continuously to be kept under control lest they return to their own homes ».

THE FALL OF THE SERENISSIMA

This situation in which Venice found herself at home could not but result in friction and actual clashes between those who had no intention of ceding their power and those who wanted to get their hands on it.
The political and economic decline of the city was strangely enough countered by a flowering of all the arts, from books to architecture. The people in this period of decline seemed to be possessed by an overwhelming love of life. There were lavish parties, a great display of wealth, a thousand excuses for entertainment. And people came from outside too to make merry, for the fame of Venice « the pleasure city » had spread beyond the borders of the Serenissima. The only ones to get anything out of it, actually, were the merchants, for whom it was not a period of decline but of plenty.
A century of neutrality had not succeeded in keeping the decadence of Venice at bay, nor was neutrality an obstacle for Napoleon when in 1796, after Montenotte, Dego, Millesimo, Mondovi and Lodi, he conquered Peschiera, an outpost fortress of Venice which constituted the object for the negotiations between Austria and France. The « *Pasque Veronesi* » (April 17, 1797) and the shelling by the Fort of Sant'Andrea of the French ship « Liberateur d'Italie », which had attempted to enter the lagoon in pursuit of a fishing boat from Chioggia, were determining factors in Napoleon's decision to attack Venice directly, ignoring the neutrality of the Republic. In fact, the general said to the deputies Donà and Giustinian who joined him in Graz: « I want no more Inquisition, I want no Senates. I will be an Attila for the Venetian state ». At this point it must be admitted that the Venetian lands suffered more when they passed to Austria than did Venice for the fall of the Serenissima, when a conspiracy of young revolutionaries, in collusion with the French consul, broke out even before the arrival of the Napoleonic troops.
The acts of servility of the new rulers and the way in which a millennial Republic had come to an end deeply disturbed the people who could not accept the fact that Venice should have a master. A master moreover who also controlled the patricians charged with public office, who had the conclave which elected Pius VII take place in San Giorgio, who sacked the Palace of the Doges destroying precious relics of the history of Venice. In the years of his reign Napoleon gave Venice little in exchange: the Chamber of Commerce, the Cemetery, the Gardens — for which he demolished an entire quarter with the churches of Sant'Antonio and of San Nicolò and the ducal seminary.
In addition, between 1806 and 1810 numerous religious communities were suppressed and seventy-two churches were torn down. In others everything was profaned: Sant'Aponal became a political prison, Santa Maria delle Vergini a penitentiary, Santa Marina a tavern. Art treasure including works by Carpaccio, the Bellinis, Tiepolo, Guardi, Tintoretto, Ricci, Pordenone were dispersed (and in great part stolen).
The period of Austrian occupation was doubtless less traumatic. It began on May 3, 1815 in the Basilica of San Marco where the representatives of the Venetian provinces swore allegiance to Francis I of Austria. A few months later the four bronze horses which Napoleon had taken to Paris were returned to the Basilica.
Venice, under Austria, became part of the Lombardo Veneto Realm as a « *città regia* » and therefore enjoyed a certain amount of autonomy in local administration. But not even in this new situation did the city manage to assume a preeminant role, not even when the benefice of « open port » was extended to the entire city.
The local economy improved after 1838 when new roads were built and the railroad Venice-Milan was begun and regular river transport along the Po was opened up. But these were also the years in which the Venetians began to demonstrate a feeling of intolerance for the Austrians. It all began within the Naval college (which was on the Canal Grande) and in the Austrian Navy itself where there were many Italian officers. Emilio and Attilio, sons of the imperial and royal Admiral Bandiera, founded « Esperia », a secret society. and attempted to take the revolt to the south. They were captured and executed in 1844 near Cosenza.
The policy adopted by Daniele Manin, descendant of the last of the doges, Ludovico, was quite different. He fully realized how impossible it would be to defeat Austria with an open rebellion, and attempted to create a vacuum around the Austrians by stressing the juridical and legislative problems. In this he was aided by the Dalmatian Nicolò Tommaseo. When the two were arrested, the conscience of the Venetians had already been awakened by the actions and speeches of the two politicans. On March 17, 1848 when the news that the Austrian chancellor Metternich had fallen as a result of the bourgeois revolt in Vienna, the Venetians staged a demonstration and asked that the two patriots be liberated. The governor Palffy, who may have been the first to maintain that their arrest was « illegal », complied immediately. It was also Palffy who asked Manin to guarantee that the troops remain in the barracks and that a civil guard be created.
Manin, Tommaseo and the head of the Civil Guard, Angelo Mengaldo, at once set to preparing a plan for future actions, concluding that Venice should once more be « independent » of all. Manin and Tommaseo lost no time in forming the new government. In the meantime in Venice an « Albertine party » had arisen which promoted annexation to Italy, a policy not shared by the two republicans Manin and Tommaseo who however did deem a temporary union with the Kingdom of Italy necessary. On August 21, Carlo Alberto's Commissioners, who had come to Venice to see how this prospective annexation could be handled, ran the risk of being lynched when the crowd heard that the king had signed the armistice of Salasco. The only road open at that point was « resisting to the bitter end » and, in only a few days, three million lire were collected from the citizens, compared to the 100,000 lire given by the national loan.
Venice however was aware that her forces were insufficient to fight an enemy as powerful as Austria, but felt it was right to take the initiative where she could, as on the occasion of the sally of Forte Marghera at Mestre. They were nothing but glorious episodes but they gave the measure of the will « to resist Austria at all costs », as Manin had said.
The end began with the abandon of Forte Marghera and with the manifestation in Venice on August 7th requesting that battle be continued. But when Manin asked to have the enlistment lists opened, only seven showed up for enlistment. On August 22nd the city capitulated and this marked the beginning of a period of domination in which, in the beginning, martial law was applied. In 1851 Luigi Dottesio was strangled in Campo di Marte; in 1852 Angelo Scarsellini, Bernardo Canal and Giacomo Zambelli were tried in Mantova and sent to the scaffold. In 1859, after the armistice of Villafranca, 4,500 people left Venice for Piedmont. After the annexation of 1866 Venice once more began to experience a period of economic recovery with important innovations in architecture and town planning.
The war of 1915-18 witnessed various bombings of Venice, such as the famous « eight-hour night » on February 27, 1918 when the Austrian reaction let loose 14,700 kilograms of bombs over Venice. The complex of Porto Marghera went up between the two great wars and the new automobile bridge between the Mainland and Venice was built.
The rest is modern history, the story of a Venice defined ever more as a center of culture and of tourism while the productive economy keeps shifting to the mainland to Mestre and Marghera, and the consequent social tension, problems of housing and immigration.

PIAZZA SAN MARCO

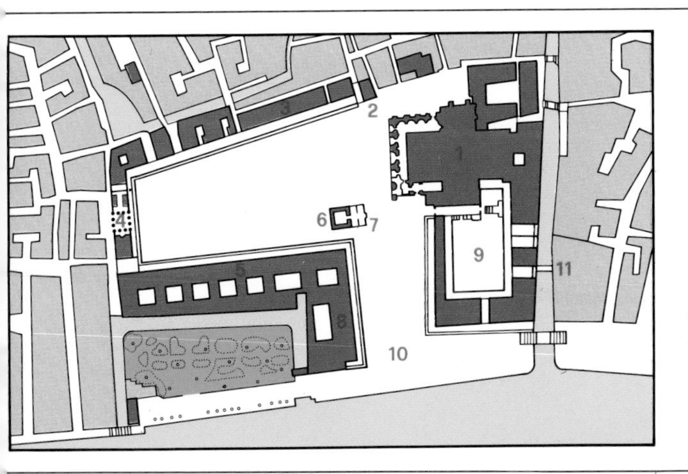

1 - Basilica of San Marco
2 - Clock Tower
3 - Procuratie Vecchie
4 - Ala napoleonica
5 - Procuratie Nuove
6 - Campanile of San Marco
7 - Sansovino's Loggetta
8 - Libreria Marciana
9 - Palace of the Doges
10 - Piazzetta San Marco
11 - Bridge of Sighs

PIAZZA SAN MARCO

A gem among gems in the field of Italian architecture, the Piazza San Marco consists of two large contiguous areas: the Piazza itself and its extension, the Piazzetta, which runs down to the sea. Unrivalled examples of architecture face out on this large open space on all sides: the **Basilica of San Marco**, the **Palace of the Doges** or Palazzo Ducale, the **Loggetta**, the tall **Clock Tower**.
The original layout of the Piazza dates to the 9th cent. A.D., and it is essentially still the same despite the various changes that have been made throughout the centuries. As early as the second half of the 12th century Doge Sebastiano Ziani modified the piazza, doubling the space in front of the Basilica, and setting up the two large monolithic columns which ideally close off the Piazzetta. A century later both the Basilica and the Palace of the Doges were variously transformed, and the fortified ducal residence became the elegant building with loggias that we see today. At the time, the Piazza was surrounded by interesting buildings such as the headquarters of the Canons of San Marco, the houses of the Procurators, and the Church of San Geminiano, with numerous shops facing out on the Piazzetta. The real transformation of the Piazza began in 1400: many buildings were torn down, the Clock Tower (late 15th cent.) was built, and the Zecca or Mint and the Library were constructed, joined a hundred years later by the Procuratie Nuove. In Sansovino's new project for the Piazza the underlying basic structures followed the original arrangement. At the beginning of the 1700s the centuries-old red brick pavement with its herringbone design was replaced with the grey trachite stone from the Euganean Hills which thousands of visitors still tread under foot today.

Two views of Piazza San Marco, the heart of Venice.

CLOCK TOWER

The Torre dell'Orologio, built by Codussi between 1496 and 1499, is undoubtedly one of the most photographed monuments in Venice, thanks both to the presence of the original clock and to the two « *Moors* » who strike the hours at the top of the tower. The construction of the lateral parts, designed by P. Lombardo, was begun in 1506 and they were raised higher in 1775 by Giorgio Massari. The bronze « *Moors* » by Ambrogio da le Anchore date to 1497.
Below the Moors is the Lion of San Marco. On the small semicircular terrace further down is a gilt copper statue of the *Madonna and Child* by A. Leopardi and during Ascension week three statues move across the terrace from left to right, passing before the Virgin. The large clock is a masterpiece of clockwork mechanism by Giampaolo and Giancarlo Ranieri from Parma (late 15th cent.), indicating the passing of the seasons, the phases of the moon and the movement of the sun from one sign of the zodiac to the other.

On these pages: various views of the Torre dell'Orologio, with the statues of the two Moors who strike the hours.

XII
25

PROCURATIE VECCHIE AND THE ALA NAPOLEONICA

The fifty round arches which support the two tiers of loggias of the Procuratie Vecchie were built between the end of the 15th and the beginning of the 16th century. M. Codussi worked on the project up to the first floor. The building was finished by B. Bon and G. Grigi, who completed almost all the rest except for the part in the back which was built by Sansovino.
A continuation of the Procuratie Vecchie, on the site of the old church of San Geminiano (demolished in 1807), is the so-called Ala Napoleonica (Napoleonic Wing), built by the French emperor as an enormous ballroom. The ala repeats the two orders of columns of the Procuratie Nuove which Scamozzi built in 1584, inspired by the classical lines of the Libreria Sansoviniana.

PROCURATIE NUOVE

When new premises for the apartments of the nine Procuratori (Magistrates) of San Marco, which were in the Procuratie Vecchie, were needed, Vincenzo Scamozzi was charged with designing the new complex of buildings. He paid little attention to a precedent project by Sansovino and took up the motive of the Libreria Marciana — which is at right angles to the Procuratie — for the two lower floors. He added an upper floor which was also articulated by semi-columns, with tall windows alternately topped by arched and triangular pediments set in between. A molded cornice runs along the entire facade at the top. The old Ospizio Orseolo, whose facade projected further out than the present Procuratie, was demolished and construction work began in

Detail of the Procuratie Vecchie.

The Procuratie Vecchie and the Ala Napoleonica (Napoleon Wing) on the right; View of the Piazza with the Procuratie Nuove and the Ala Napoleonica, below.

1582 under the direction of Scamozzi. At his death in 1616 work was continued by Carità and then terminated by Longhena. These rooms were turned into the Royal Palace for Napoleon when he was in Venice. Now the nine apartments of the Procuratori, overlooking five inner courtyards, house the **Archaeological Museum**, the **Museo Civico Correr** and the **Museo del Risorgimento**, as well as various municipal offices. The public establishments on the ground floor include, under the portico, the **Caffè Florian**, once the « Venezia trionfante », the meeting place of artists and writers in the 18th and 19th centuries.

CAMPANILE OF SAN MARCO

The Piazza San Marco is dominated by the lofty bell tower about 100 meters high called « *el paron de casa* » (the master of the house) by the Venetians. But it did not always look like this. In the 9th century, a lookout tower stood on the site which at the time faced directly onto the lagoon since the Piazzetta San Marco (now between the Libreria Marciana and the Palace of the Doges) was a sort of inner harbor. Rebuilt in the second half of the 12th century, two sides of the campanile were at the time set against the buildings which stood in front of the present Procuratie Nuove (the Ospizio Orseolo) and in the area of the Libreria, constituting the corner.
Frequently damaged, it was rebuilt between 1511 and 1514 by Bartolomeo Bon on a project by Giorgio Spavento. Set apart from the adjacent buildings, the shaft of the powerful stocky tower has pilasters up to the arches which make it look like a pier of the classic period. Over the belfry, pierced by four-light openings, is a drum which supports the pyramidal steeple and the statue of the Archangel Gabriel. Inaugurated with great pomp, the structure stood intact until 1902, when it suddenly crumbled. It was decided to rebuild it « *com'era e dov'era* » (as it was and where it was). Reconstruction terminated in 1912, including Sansovinos Loggetta which had been gravely damaged when the bell tower fell. Nowadays, from the belfry where Galileo tried out his telescope, a magnificent panorama can be had over the lagoon and the city as far as the Alps.

SANSOVINO'S LOGGETTA

The Loggetta was designed by Sansovino for the base of the campanile. In the niches the architect placed bronze statues of *Apollo*, *Mercury*, *Peace*, and *Minerva*. The *gate* and the two *putti* on either side of the attic are by A. Gai.
In 1505 A. Leopardo set up three *standard bases* between the Loggia and the Clock Tower to replace their wooden forebears. The one in the center has a medallion with the profile of *Doge L. Loredan*.

Two pictures of the famous Campanile and a detail of Sansovino's graceful Loggetta.

ISTITUTO ITALIANO PER GLI STUDI FILOSOFICI
ACCADEMIA NAZIONALE DEI LINCEI
FEDERICO CESI
E LA FONDAZIONE DELL'ACCADEMIA DEI LINCEI

LIBRERIA MARCIANA

The entire west side of the Piazzetta San Marco is occupied by the Libreria Marciana or Sansovino Library. The palace was destined to house the precious collection of books which Cardinal Bessarione had gratefully donated to the city for having given him asylum when he fled from Nicea (where he was bishop) when it was occupied by the Turks. The building, which consists of two stories — a Doric portico and an Ionic upper story —, was commissioned from Sansovino by the Senate of the Republic in 1536. Two large caryatids flank the central entrance in the portico. Inside, at the top of a remarkable staircase in two flights which imitates the « golden staircase » in the Doges' Palace, is a vestibule with a splendid ceiling decorated by Stefano and Cristoforo Rosa in the middle of the 16th century.
The library contains outstanding treasures from the Biblioteca Marciana including the famous *Grimani Breviary*, a precious illuminated codex of the Flemish school, and the well-known *Mappamento di Fra Mauro* (1549), a map on vellum by Fra Mauro. In addition to hundreds of thousands of books for consultation and study, the Library also has rare examples of Greek and Latin codexes, as well as Marini Sanudo's « *Diari* » (« *Afamato curioso di notizie* » as he defined himself — famished for curious facts).
The Zecca or Mint where the famous gold zecchino was coined is also by Sansovino. The palace was taken over by the Libreria Marciana in 1905.

BASILICA OF SAN MARCO

an Marco is the « great temple » of Venice, the monumen-al symbol not only of the State Church, but of political power as well, for it was originally created as a Ducal Chapel and did not become the seat of the Patriarch until the 19th century. The Procurators of San Marco, entrusted both with the burden and the honor of looking after the Basilica, were not members of the clergy, and the « Primicerio », a noble of the Republic, to whom canons and vicars turned their eyes during the religious rites, was chosen by the doge. San Marco was the heart of the city, the fulcrum around which life in Venice revolved. It was here that the newly elected doge was solemnly acclaimed and it was in the Basilica that the doge blessed and solemnly saw off those who had been charged with leading the ships and armies of the Most Serene Republic into war.

The *doorways* set into the *facade* of the Basilica of San Marco are five in number, just as there are five cupolas in eastern style which lend both solidity and movement to the structure as a whole. Each of the portals presents specific moments in the story of the *Recovery of the Body of the Evangelist*. Beginning on the right, we have the *Body of St. Mark Stolen from the Infidels*, the *Arrival in Venice of the Mortal Remains of the Saint* (by Pietro Vecchia), then the *Venetians Worshipping the Body of St. Mark* (the mosaic is by Sebastiano Ricci), and the *Translation of the Body of St. Mark to the Church*. The central portal is decorated with bas

The Basilica of San Marco, the principle monument in the city.

The Libreria Marciana.

Some of the principal monuments in the city look out on the Piazzetta San Marco.

Detail of the principal portal with the mosaic by Liber
Salandri (1836) depicting Christ in Glory and the La
Judgemen

Detail of the facade of the Basilica of San Marco.

Detail of the portal of San Alipio with the mosaic depictin
the Translation of the Body of Saint Mark in the Basilic

VT VENETOS SEMPER SERVET AB HOSTE SVOS
IC XC

Basilica of San Marco, atrium. Above: general view of the left side; below: detail of the center of the so-called "Genesis" dome with the mosaics depicting the creation of man. Facing page: the building of the Tower of Babel.

reliefs in Venetian Romanesque style representing the *Vene-tian Trades*, the *Months* and the *Virtues*. The large mosai above is a 19th-century work after a cartoon by Lattanzi and depicts the *Last Judgement*.
Further up, behind a slender balustrade, are copies of th *four horses* attributed to Lysippus, of the 4th century B.C brought back from Constantinople in 1204 as spoils of wa by Doge Enrico Dandolo.
The horses were placed on San Marco in 1250. In 179 Napoleon took them to Paris as war booty but in 1815 the were returned to Venice thanks to the Austrians. The orig-nals, duly restored, are now inside the church.
Four octagonal columns with 11th-century capitals are ir-stalled behind these imposing bronze horses. All the sculp-ture in the upper part was begun in 1385 by the Dal Masegne.
The facade that overlooks the *Piazzetta dei Leoncini*, s named for the two lions in red marble, and where th vegetable market was held, echoes the design of the mai facade, with arches and marble statues in the aedicules an gables. The bas reliefs and the water spouts, by Pietro Lam-berti, are also quite lovely, as is the elegant *Porta dei Fior* inserted in the fourth arcade. Under a large arch on th

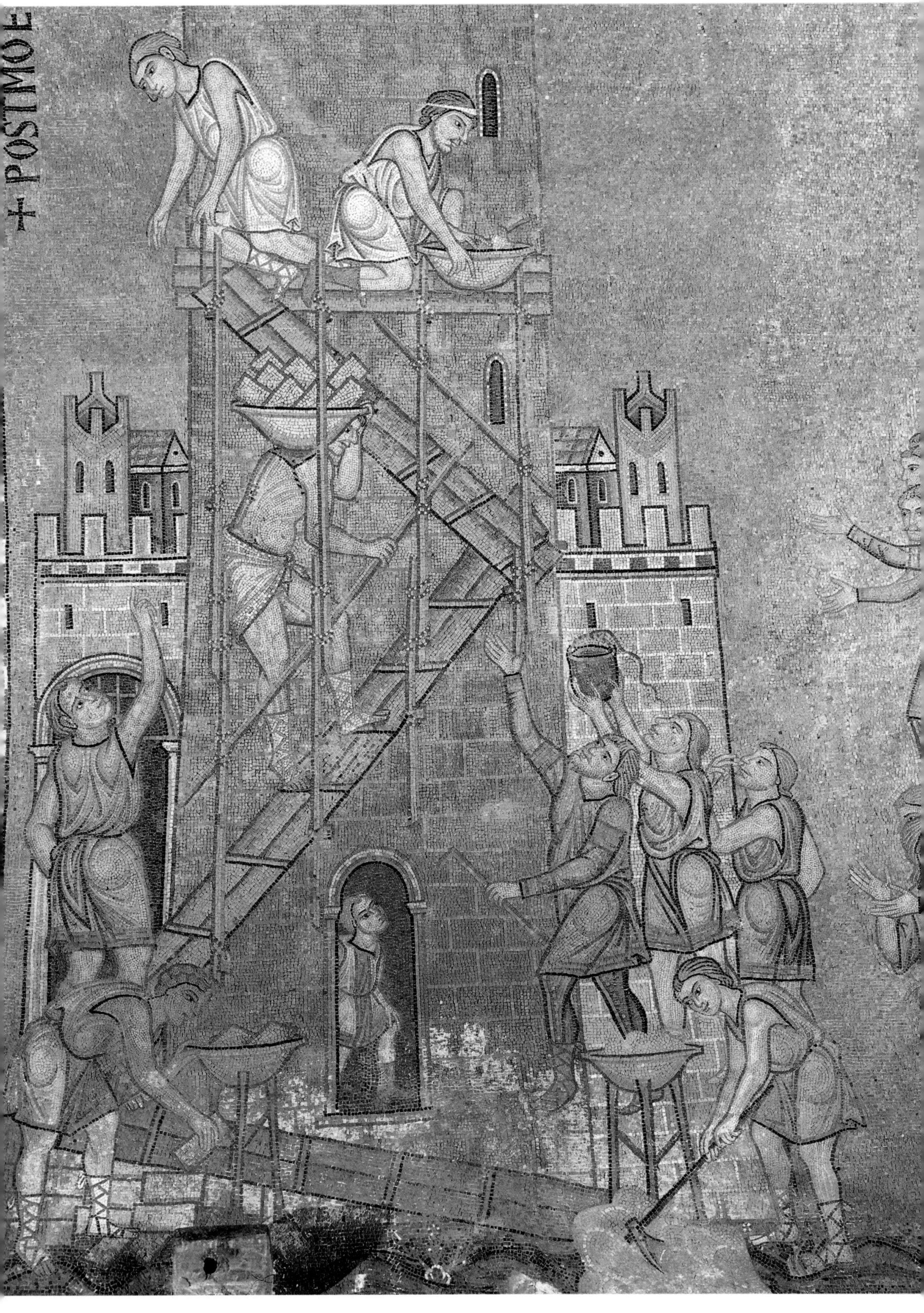
+ POSTMOE

General view of the interior.

View of the rood screen in polychrome marble and the great Cross in gilded bronze made in 1393 by the Venetian goldsmith Jacopo di Marco Benato. On the left, the double ambo dating to the 14th century.

same side is the *tomb of Daniele Manin*, by Luigi Borro, whose mortal remains were brought back from Paris in 1868.
The lovely Baroque facade (1675) of the ex-church of **San Basso** — attributed to Longhena — also faces onto this square. Inside are the four panels from the organ of San Marco by Giovanni Bellini. At the back of the piazza the neo-classic facade of the **Palazzo Patriarcale**, a 19th-century building by Lorenzo Santi, stands in all its clarity of form.
A spacious **atrium** and a sort of gallery that runs the entire length of the church separate the outside from the inside of the Basilica. These sixty-two meters (6 m. wide and 7.35 m. high) of wall are decorated with columns from various places. Some of them, according to legend, are said to come from Solomon's Temple. The pavement is in marble mosaic. The arches are decorated with mosaics depicting *Scenes from the Old and New Testaments*, most of which were made by Venetian craftsmen after cartoons by Pietro Vecchia, Salviati, Titian and Pordenone.
The *tombs of Marino Morosini* (1253), *Bartolomeo Gradenigo* (1342) and *Felicita Falier* (1101) are also to be found in the atrium. A marble slab indicates the point where Frede ick Barbarossa kneeled before Pope Alexander III on Jul 23, 1177.
The *interior* of San Marco is in the form of a Greek cros with five great hemispherical cupolas, one over each arm c the cross and one in the center. Galleries run along the in terior of the church which is 76.50 meters long includin the atrium and 62.60 m. wide at the transept. The centra cupola is 43 meters high outside and 28.25 meters high in side.
In the left aisle at the end of the left transept is the **Chape of the Madonna dei Mascoli** which belonged to a Confrater nity of men only. The altar in flamboyant Gothic and datec 1430 is attributed to Giovanni Bon. The mosaics, variousl attributed, fuse the old Venetian school with the Renais sance.
The **Altar of the Madonna Nicopeia** on the right aisle of th left transept preserves the famous image of the *Virgin of Vic tory*, a Byzantine painting with enamels which may date t the 10th century and which was brought to Venice fron Constantinople in 1204 by Enrico Dandolo together witl the famous bronze horses. Facing out onto the nave of th

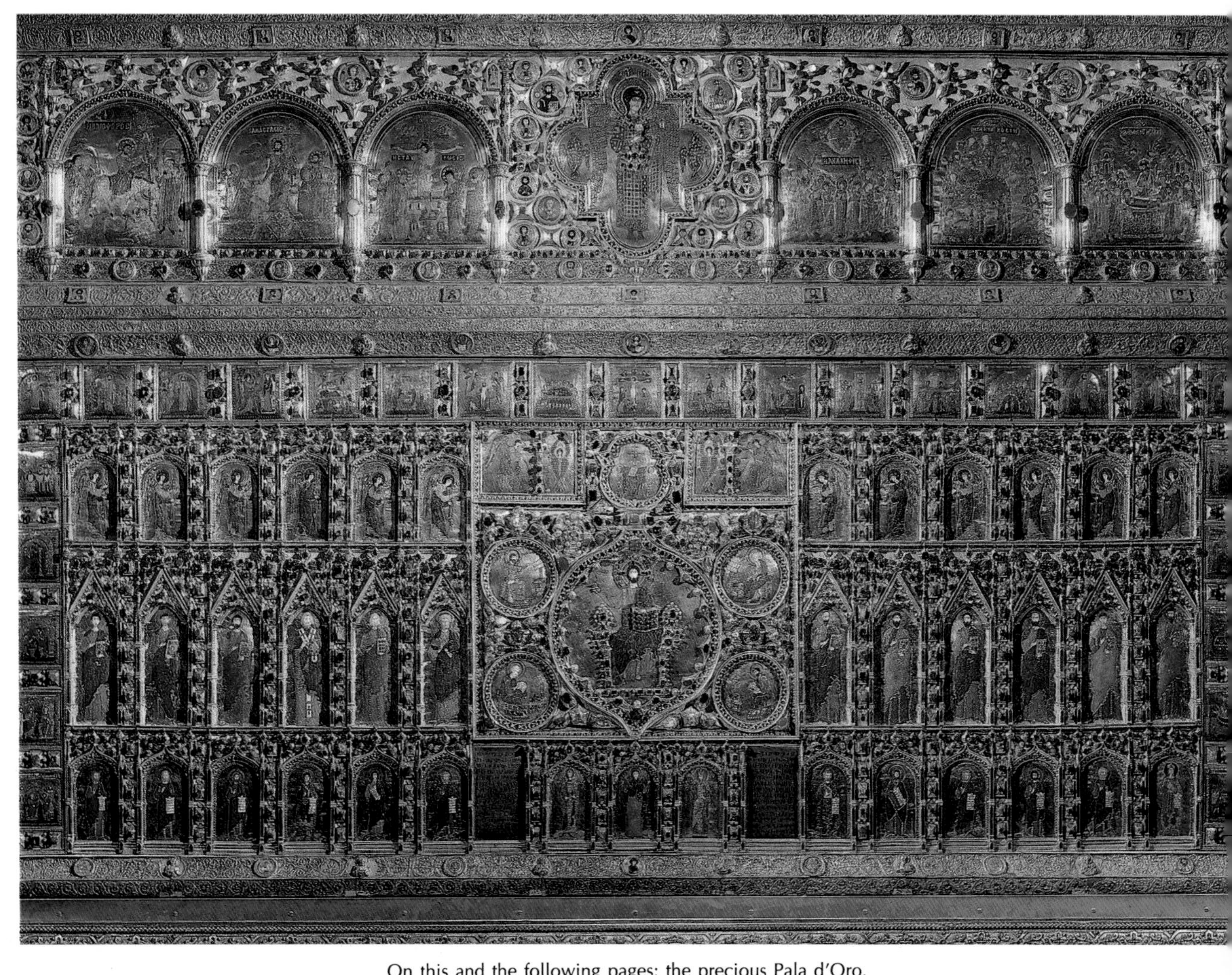

On this and the following pages: the precious Pala d'Oro.

The Pala d'Oro: detail of the lower register with the figure of a Saint executed in enamel and precious stones.

Two details of the decoration of the alabaster columns of the high altar: left, the astrologer and a prophet; on the right, a story inspired by the Gospels. Both are the work of Venetian craftsmen around 1250.

Two pictures of the mosaic pavement with its polychrome tesseras, with geometric motives and the figure of a rhinocerous.

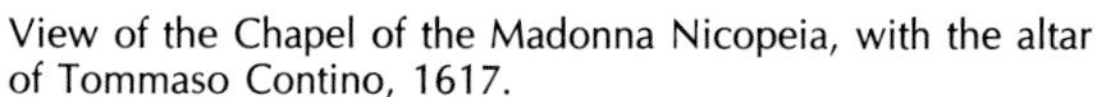

View of the Chapel of the Madonna Nicopeia, with the altar of Tommaso Contino, 1617.

The Chapel of St. Isidore, in polychrome marble with the vault covered with 14th-century mosaics.

View of the altar of the Sacrament in the central apse, showing the twisted alabaster columns and the door of the Ciborium by Sansovino.

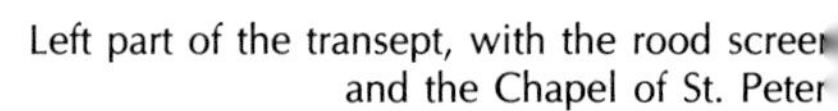

Left part of the transept, with the rood screen and the Chapel of St. Peter

transept at the pier of the crossing is the **Altar of St. Paul** an exquisite Renaissance creation.
The Sanctuary or Chancel is raised to allow for the crypt underneath, where the body of Saint Mark was once kept (now under the High Altar). The **Chapel of St. Peter**, to the left of the chancel, has statues by the Dalle Masegne brothers, a Gothic reliquary shrine, and *St. Andrew* and *St. Matthew* in mosaic on the underside of the arch overhead as well as a 13th-century mosaic of *St. Peter*.
Two doors behind the altar lead to the **Sacristy** and the small **Church of St. Theodore**. Some of the mosaics in the vault of the Sacristy are by Titian. The former church of St Theodore was once the chapel of the Holy Office and has a splendid *Nativity*, an early work by G. B. Tiepolo, of 1732. Access to the apse is also from the Chapel of St. Peter. In the semidome of the apse is a 16th-century restoration of a mosaic of the *Blessing Christ*. Between the windows are the vestiges of the oldest mosaics in the Basilica which survived the fire of 1106. The *bronze doors* leading to the Sacristy are by Sansovino.

QVIA IVSTI
S PETICION
NTRADICE
PRIVILEGII

The famous Horses of the Basilica of San Marco.

The *high altar* stands under a ciborium supported by four columns of oriental alabaster. The reliefs on the columns are by 13th-century Venetian artists. On top are the statues of the *Redeemer* and the *Evangelists*. On either side of the ciborium are four statues: the *Evangelists* by Jacopo Sansovino on the left, and the *Doctors of the Church* by Girolamo Paliari on the right.
Behind the altar is the famous scintillating **Gold Altar Screen**, the **Pala d'Oro**, a masterpiece of the goldsmith's art, 3.48 meters wide and 1.40 meters high. It was originally ordered by Doge Pietro Orseolo I (976-978) in Constantinople and was enriched in 1105 with gold and enamels brought from the Monastery of the Pantocrater at the time of the IV Crusade. It was later radically rearranged by Boninsegna. Some of the outstanding enamels include those depicting episodes from the *Life of Christ* and of *St. Mark* and the *Virgin*.
The cupola of the chancel is clothed with mosaics representing the *Religion of Christ foretold by the Prophets* Separating the sanctuary from the body of the church is a marble iconostasis or rood screen, consisting of eight marble columns which support an architrave with fourteen statues. The mosaics in the great arch above represent scenes from the *Life of Christ* after cartoons by Jacopo Tintoretto. The Doge and the high magistrates of the Republic took part in the religious functions from the sanctuary.
The **Chapel of St. Clement** has statues by the Dalle Masegne. From a small grated window, set to the right of the altar, the Doge could take part in the mass privately from the Ducal Palace.
The **Treaury of San Marco** is preceded by the Sanctuary in which 110 reliquaries and various religious paraphernalia are preserved. The Treasury proper contains the relics and precious objects that the Venetians have donated to the Republic throughout the centuries.
The **Baptistery** is called the Chiesa dei Putti (Church of the

abies) by the Venetians. It contains the funeral monument f Doge *Andrea Dandolo* and the sarcophagus of *Doge iovanni Soranzo*. The *baptismal font* was designed in 545 by Sansovino, whose mortal remains are under the ombstone by the altar. In the cupolas and in the vaults are 4th-century mosaics of the Venetian school. The **Zen hapel** is dedicated to Cardinal G. B. Zen who left a substantial legacy to the city when he died. On the bronze altar – in Lombardesque style — stands the *Madonna of the hoe*, so-called because of a legend in which a poor man ave a shoe to the Madonna which was changed to gold. hirteenth-century mosaics narrate episodes from the *Life of t. Mark*.

The entrance to the **Marciano Museum** or Museum of San Marco is next to the central door of the Church. The Museum is composed of a vast and precious collection of works of art, lace, carpets, and tapestries. The *organ doors* painted by Gentile Bellini are quite remarkable, as are the tapestries made to designs by Sansovino. The Museum also contains the *polyptych* by P. Veneziano which was formerly a case for the Pala d'Oro.

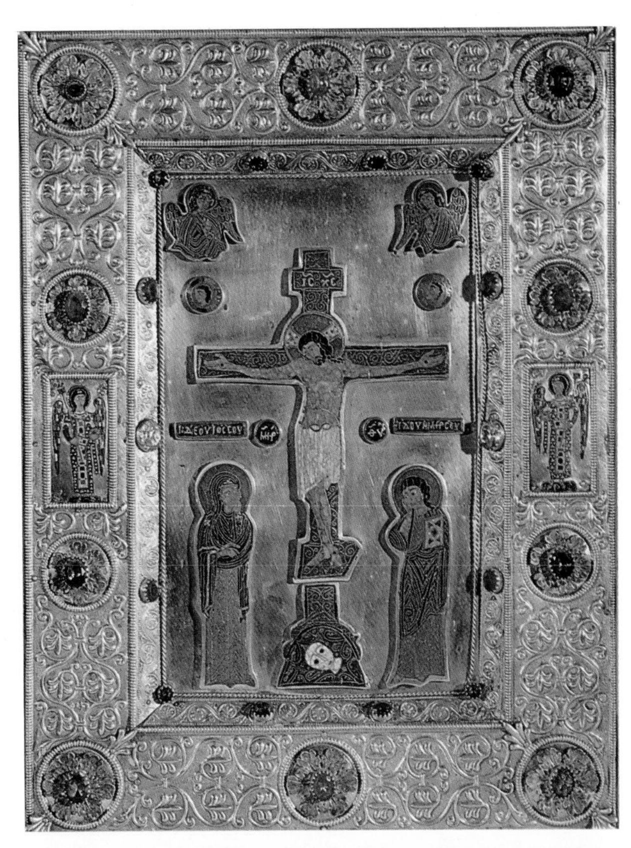

Treasury of San Marco: Icon of the Crucifixion (Byzantine art, 12th cent. ca.).

A mosaic in the Baptistery depicting the Dance of Salome (Venetian school — mid-14th century).

View from the top of the Palazzo Ducale or Palace of the Doges.

PALACE OF THE DOGES

The first Ducal Palace, or palace for the Doge, which could be more easily defended from enemy attacks via sea, could not have been built until at least a year or two after the government moved its headquarters from Malamocco to Venice at the beginning of the 9th century.
In the second half of the 12th century Sebastiano Ziani, elected doge in 1172, decided to enlarge the original palace and the building took shape along the lines of its present ground plan.
Presumably this new building was more like a castle than a palace; in other words it was equipped with towers and defenses. In 1177 when Frederick Barbarossa came to Venice to be reconciled with Pope Alexander II he was a guest here. As the economic and commercial power of the State grew, the time came when the extant structures were no longer sufficient. In 1301 Doge Pietro Gradenigo decided to have a new palace built which would include a hal for the legislative assemblies and for the offices of the Chancellery.
With a decree of 1340 the construction of the Sala del Maggior Consiglio was established. Work began with the facade towards the lagoon and the first six arches on the Piazzetta Chronicles report that the work was entrusted to Pietro Baseggio and his son-in-law Filippo Calendario.
The large spacious window overlooking the lagoon was commissioned by Doge Michele Steno from Jacobello and Pier Paolo Dalle Masegne in 1404, as witnessed by the date engraved at the top of the parapet. It is a beautiful example of flamboyant Gothic. The rest of the wing where the window was opened must have been built about forty years earlier, for in 1365 Guariento from Padua had been called in to fresco the upper hall with a *Paradise*. The difference

etween the wing on the waterfront and the old Ziani wing n the Piazzetta led the Venetian Senate to decide to emolish the latter and complete the whole palace in the tyle of the former. The construction was entrusted to iiovanni and Bartolomeo Bon and began on March 27, 424 when Francesco Foscari was doge. Work was unquesonably terminated before 1457. In the same period (1438-442) the so-called Porta della Carta, first known as Grande » and then « Dorata », was built between the alazzo and the Basilica.

1 1483 a raging fire destroyed the chapel, various rooms nd the golden hall of the « Maps ». Antonio Rizzo from Vena was charged with the reconstruction and during the fteen years he spent on the job he designed the *Scala dei iiganti*, the facades on the courtyard and towards the Rio i Palazzo. In April of 1498 however he was accused of aud and had to flee from Venice and the work was then ntrusted to the « *proto* » (head architect) Pietro Solari nown as Lombardo. Jacopo Sansovino finished the east ving between the Cortiletto dei Senatori (Senators' Courtard), by the Basilica, and the original building overlooking ne lagoon.

nother conflagration broke out on May 11, 1574, damagng the halls of the College and the Anticollege. Still another re on December 10, 1577 ravaged the Halls of the Magior Consiglio and the Scrutinio, destroying works by Bellii, Carpaccio, Veronese and Tintoretto. With Antonio Da onte in charge of rebuilding, the palace was restored to its riginal forms within the eight months promised.

Externally the upper part of the building is not nearly as airy as the lower part. From the Porta della Carta up to the Ponte della Paglia, the ground-floor portico with its pointed arches and columns without pedestals is echoed, on the floor above, by the long loggia with ogee arches and quadrilobate tracery. The upper floor, illuminated by large pointed-arch windows, is set above this loggia. The narrow crowning cornice is topped by airy oriental cresting. Openwork aedicules are on the corners.

After the fire of 1577, a statue of *Venice in the guise of Justice* by Alessandro Vittoria was set on the large window overlooking the waterfront. The niches at the sides have a figure of *St. Theodore*, and one of *St. George* by Antonio Canova. The window in the facade towards the Piazzetta was opened in 1537 after designs by Jacopo Sansovino. His pupils sculptured the statues of *Neptune* and *Mars* in the niches on either side. Above the balcony is a relief depicting *Doge Andrea Gritti kneeling before the winged Lion*, a copy by Ugo Bottasso of the original which was destroyed in the revolutionary uprisings of 1797. Crowning the window is a figure of *Justice* by Alessandro Vittoria (1579). Both the columns of the ground-floor portico and those of the loggia have sculptured capitals. The finest are those on the side facing the lagoon, since those on the Piazzetta are in part copies.

Particularly fine is the capital on the seventeenth column, counting from the corner at Ponte della Paglia, with the *Wise Men*, and also the seventh on the Piazzetta (starting at the waterfront) with *Marriage*, where the sculptor describes

he Porta della Carta and the Finestra Ducale.

Following pages: the Palace of the Doges in all its majesty and beauty.

fascinating view of the courtyard of the Palace of the Doges.

The Doges' Courtyard.

he life span of man and the marriage and domestic customs of the time in eight scenes, analytically describing the costumes worn by the Venetians in the 14th century.
here are also two scenes set one above the other at the corners of the facades. In the corner by the Ponte della Paglia the *Drunkenness of Noah* is below and the *Archangel Raphael and Tobias* are on the loggia at the corner of the Piazzetta on the waterfront, *Adam and Eve* are on the corner column and the *Archangel Michael* on the loggia. The corner towards the Basilica has the *Judgement of Solomon* below (attributed to Pietro Lamberti or Nanni di Bartolo) and above the Archangel Gabriel by Bartolomeo Bon.
The **Porta della Carta** is one of the two main entrances to the palace. The other is the **Porta del Frumento** (Wheat Door) on the waterfront. A third entrance (the **Porta dell'Armar**) was opened on the Piazzetta in 1610. The name « della Carta » (of the paper) seems to derive from the fact that notices of the governmental decrees were posted here (or perhaps it was because the State Archives were nearby). The public scribes also seem to have had their stalls there. It is the work of Giovanni and Bartolomeo Bon, although what we see now is a radical 19th- century restoration, after the havoc wreaked in 1797. *Temperance* and *Fortitude* in the two lower niches are attributed to Antonio Rizzo. The figures of *Prudence* and *Charity*, in the upper niches, are also by the Bon family. Both the Porta della Carta and the Porta del Frumento give access to the **Courtyard** which is a finely balanced ensemble of works made over a range of 200 years, from the 15th to the 17th century. There are two bronze *well-heads* in the center, by the master casters Alfonso Alberghetti (1559) (the one near the Foscari Porch) and by Nicolò Costi (1556) for the other. Right across from the entrance of the Porta della Carta (the so-called **Foscari Arch** begun by the Bons and completed by A. Rizzo and by

FEDERICO CESI
ONDAZIONE DELL'ACCADEMIA DEI LINCEI

The Doges' Courtyard: the Scala dei Giganti, or Giants' Staircase, a view of the colonnade of the gallery, one of the two well-heads and the Foscari Arch with the statue of Francesco I della Rovere, of 1587.

Bregno) is the **Scala dei Giganti** or Giants' Staircase with the statues of *Mars* and *Neptune* by Sansovino. The coronation ceremony of the doge used to take place at the top of the Scala on a landing with arches, at the level of the first floor. After having sworn allegiance to the Most Serene Republic (« promissione ducale ») the doge was crowned by the oldest of the ducal Councilors. At the foot of the staircase, on the side facing the Basilica, is the **Cortiletto dei Senatori** where it is said the Senators assembled for particular ceremonies.

The east facade of the building was by Antonio Rizzo who began it after the fire of 1483. After his flight, the work was terminated by Pietro Lombardo. The part of the facade facing the Scala d'Oro was carried out by Scarpagnino (on designs by Rizzo). The **facades** to the south and west date to the early 17th century and were built under the direction of the *proto* Bartolomeo Manopola, eliminating the stables and the prisons. On the north side of the courtyard (also known as the Clock facade) there was once another staircase called the Scala Foscara or « del Piombo » because it was covered with lead plates. At the beginning of the 17th century it was demolished to make way for the new construction with the statue of the *Duke of Urbino* given to Venice by his nephew Francesco Maria della Rovere II.

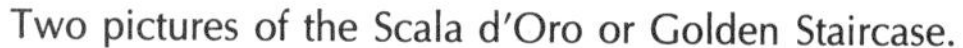

Two pictures of the Scala d'Oro or Golden Staircase.

The Room of the Four Doors: a detail of the ceiling and view of the room. The painting on the left shows the Arriva of Henry III in Venice

The **loggia** on the first floor, which runs along three sides of the interior and two facades on the exterior, was built to provide access to all the offices of the various magistrates. An inscription by Vittoria on the loggia at the top of the Giants' Staircase refers to the visit the King of France, Henri III, made to Venice in 1574. Under the inscription is one of the many « lion's mouths » into which secret denunciations were inserted. The doorway to the right of the inscription leads to the **Hall of the lower Chancellory**, office of the « segretario alle voci » whose task it was to keep the registers of the offices and the proclamations for the elections. Then comes the **Stanza dei Provveditori alla Milizia da Mar**, a magistrature instituted in 1571 charged with raising an armed navy capable of defeating the Turks. As time passed their field of competence grew, eventually including the exacting of the « tithe », a tax of 10% on the wages of those in the pay of the Republic as well as of private individuals.

The **First Room** and the **Second Room of the Avogaria** were the offices of the Avogadori de Comun, fiscal lawyers comparable to a district attorney. They were also entrusted with the « Libro d'Oro » (Book of Gold) and the « Libro d'Argento » (Book of Silver), respectively listing the nobility and the bourgeoisie. Through a corridor it was possible to go from the second hall to the **Bridge of Sighs**, and from there to the **Prisons** which had two sections: the « piombi » and the « pozzi ». The latter (the wells), were situated at the level of the lagoon and were for those who had committed more serious crimes.

The **Scala d'Oro** or Golden Staircase, begun in 1583 on a design by Sansovino and completed by Scarpagnino in 1559, was a true ceremonial staircase used by the doge on his way to official ceremonies. Two doors open off the staircase which was reserved to illustrious personages and magistrates (one branch leads to the apartments of the doge). These doors lead to the **Sala degli Scudieri** (Pages Room) and the **Sala del Magistrato al Criminal**.

The square drawing-room at the top of the Stairs contains works by J. Tintoretto (ceiling), Paolo Veronese and F. Bassano (on the walls). The left door leads to the **Cancelleria Ducale Superiore** and to the **Gran Cancelleria**, the one on the right to the **Room of the Four Doors** (delle Quattro

View of the Sala dell'Anticollegio, or Waiting Room.

The Lion of San Marco, painting by Vittore Carpacci

Two paintings in the Sala dell'Anticollegio: the Rape of Europa by Paolo Veronese and the Discovery of Arianne by Tintoretto.

Porte), a sort of antichamber for the **Anticollegio** and the **Collegio**. The former was used by those who were to be received by the doge in the « collegio », the latter was where the encounters of the doge with the Signoria della Serenissima, the Salvi Grandi and those of « Terraferma ed agli ordini » (comprising the full College) took place. It was where affairs of State were discussed.

The corridor next to the *throne* leads to the **Antichiesetta** (Antichapel), a sort of passageway to the **Secret Archives** and the **Ufficio del Savio Cassiere**. In the Chiesetta or Chapel the doge participated in mass every day, entering through the door to the right of the altar which communicates with stairs going down to the apartment on the floor below.

The **Andito del Consiglio dei Dieci** and the following **Sala del Consiglio** (Hall of the Council of Ten) are also reached from the Room of the Four Doors. Next in line is the so-called **Hall of the Bussola** which takes its name from the screened-off wooden box in the right corner. It is to all extents the interior of the « Bocca di Leone » (Lion's Mouth) and was where the Fante dei Cai (the chief of Police) used to wait. The next room is that of the **Three Heads of the Consiglio dei Dieci**, chosen every month by the Council from its Ten members. The **Room of the State Inquisitors** is reached from here and then two corridors lead to the Prisons.

The corridor after the lefthand doorway of the Hall of the Bussola leads both to the **Hall of the Censors** and to the **Armeria** where what was salvaged from the destruction of 1797 has been collected in three halls (dedicated to Gattamelata, Morosini and Bragadin). The door at the back of the last hall leads to the doge's apartments consisting of various rooms. The doge's councilors waited in the **Sala degli Scarlatti** (named after the color of their robes). During his term of office, the arms of the prince were exhibited in the **Sala dello Scudo** or delle **Carte Geografiche**, and this is also where his bodyguards waited. The coat of arms now shown is that of the last doge, Ludovico Manin. The **Sala dei Filosofi** or Philosophers' Hall from which the doge had access to the stairs which led to the chapel owes its name to the

Two pictures of the Sala del Collegio.

A view of the Sala del Senato and a detail of the ceiling wit
the allegory of the League of Cambrai

twelve *Philosophers* painted by Veronese and Tintoretto, se in the walls before they were returned to the Libreria Vec chia (Sansovino Library). The **Sala degli Stucchi**, reachec from the last door on the left, contains paintings by variou masters, including Jacopo Tintoretto and G. B. Veneziano A door next to the fireplace (now walled up) led to the **Ban quet Hall**. After the passage is the **Sala Erizzo**, a receptior hall, followed by the **Sala Grimani** with a fine fireplace by the Lombardos.
Retracing one's steps and therefore recrossing the twc rooms just described, we pass into the **Hall of the Quaran- tia Vecchia ai Civil** and the **Guariento Room** which was ar

The Great Council Chamber.

The Sala della Quarantia Civil Vecchia and the Sala della Quarantia Criminale.

arms deposit for the Maggior Consiglio. The remains of the *Paradise* painted by Guariento and damaged in the fire of 1577 are to be found here. The passage then leads to the **Sala del Maggior Consiglio**, or the Great Council Chamber, 54 m. long and 25 m. wide. All the nobles listed in the Libro d'oro who were over 25 years old automatically had the right to a seat, as well as thirty patricians between 25 and 30 years of age who were drawn by lot every year on the day of St. Barbara. An enormous canvas 7.65 m. by 24.6 m. dominates the back wall. Tintoretto painted it between 1588 and 1590 in the Scuola Vecchia della Misericordia. It has been restored more than once. Works by Veronese, Palma Giovane, A. Vicentini are also in the hall, on three sides of which runs a frieze with the *portraits of the doges*, two by two, painted by D. Tintoretto. Until 1902 many of the books of the Biblioteca Marciana were housed here.

The staircase that begins at the **Triumphal Arch** (honoring Doge Morosini, the Peloponnesiacus) leads down to the **Loggia Foscara** with a fine view of the Basilica, the Piazzetta, and the quay. This was where exhibitions were organized by the Congregations of Arts and Trades when the doge and dogaressa were crowned. The inner loggia (on the

Three famous doges: Alvise Contarini, Marcantonio Trevisan and Marcantonio Bragadin.

courtyard) then leads to the **Hall of the Censors**, a magistra-ture created in 1507 to keep an eye on possible election frauds. Access to the **Palazzo delle Prigioni** where the rooms have vaults in Istrian stone is from this room. A wooden staircase then leads to the « pozzi » or « wells » where the cells were marked with Roman numerals. The only cell that survived the destruction of 1797 is Roman numeral VII still lined with wooden boards, a pallet in larch wood, and a small shelf.
The **Museo dell'Opera di Palazzo** on the ground floor has the original capitals from the exterior colonnade of the Doges' Palace (replaced during restoration), some columns reliefs and original fragments from the crenellation and the architrave of the Porta della Carta.

DENONTIE SECRETE
CONTRO CHI OCCVLTERA
GRATIE ET OFFICII
O COLLVDERA PER
NASCONDER LA VERA
RENDITA D ESSI

The Lion's Mouth for anonymous accusations.

The entrance corridor to the Prigioni Nuove.

The interior of a cell in the prisons known as "i Pozzi", the "Wells".

THE BRIDGE OF SIGHS

This small bridge over the Rio di Palazzo is one of the bes known monuments in the city and a must for the sight-see Its fame depends not so much on its architecture as it doe on the 19th-century writers who often referred to it in thei works and baptized it by this name. To tell the truth, in pas centuries it must really have been a melancholy passage fo those forced to cross it on their way from the prisons to th court or on their way back to the narrow dark cells of th Prigioni Nuove of the Most Serene Republic.
The prisons were built between the 16th and 17th centurie on the other side of the Rio di Palazzo. Doge Marino Grima ni then ordered the construction of a bridge to connect th place of confinement with the rooms of the Quarantia, th Tribunale and the Avogaria via two narrow superposed pas sageways. Built around 1602, possibly designed by Antoni

The famous Bridge of Sighs or Ponte dei Sospiri

The palace of the Doges seen from the Grand Canal.

The Drunkenness of Noah carved on the Doge's Palace at the corner of the Rio di Palazzo.

The Palace of the Doges and the Ponte della Paglia.

The famous Venetian gondolas

Contin, the bridge is characterized by the exceptional height at which it is set and by the fact that it is completely covered, both overhead and at the sides. The edges of the arch are decorated with heads and over the span is a horizontal band articulated with rusticated pilaster strips and two small tracery windows in between. Further up a low-arched pediment with a relief of *Justice* seated between two lions is set under volutes.

ISOLE
MURANO
TORCELLO

The Ponte della Paglia and the Palace of the Prigioni Nuove.

Two views of the Riva degli Schiavor

RIVA DEGLI SCHIAVONI

Ever since the 19th century when Napoleon had the Public Gardens installed near the eastern extremity, the Riva degli Schiavoni has been one of the typical promenades of the Venetians (and non-Venetians). Even before then the zone was buzzing with activity for as early as the 11th century this was where the boats moored, unloading and selling their merchandise here, work done mostly by sailors from Dalmatia (Schiavonia or Slav-land).
After the 14th-century **Ponte della Paglia**, near which the straw for the stables and the pallets of the prisoners of the Republic was unloaded, come the **Prigioni Nuove**, built between the 16th and 17th centuries and communicating with the back of th Palazzo Ducale via the Bridge of Sighs. Further on is the 15th-century **Palazzo Dandolo**, now Hotel Danieli, where kings and unforgettable figures such as D Musset, Wagner, D'Annunzio, Dickens, and Balzac staye
After the **Ponte del Vin** and the **Ponte della Pietà**, comes th **Church of the Pietà**, rebuilt between 1745 and 1760 b Massari and annexed to the **Hospital of the Pietà** or of th Esposti. The church houses prestigious works of sculptu and painting, including the *Coronation of the Virgin* b Giovanbattista Tiepolo, while the hostel, whose foundatio elsewhere, dates back to 1348, was the theater of Antoni Vivaldi's activity between 1703 and 1740.
Other monuments to be mentioned on the Riva deg Schiavoni include the former **Monastery of the Santo Sepo cro**, once a hostel for pilgrims on their way to the Holy Lan and a monastery between 1745 and 1806, and the **Palazz Gabrieli**, now a hotel, a 14th-century structure with a reli of the *Archangel Gabriel* on the facade and an elegant *wel head* in the courtyard.

DANIELI EXCELSIOR

DANIELI
SAVOIA & JOLANDA

GRAND CANAL

This long water-way (almost 4 kilometers) crosses just about all the city. Travelling along the canal is one way of seeing the highlights of Venice, for many of the most prestigious palaces line either side. The canal winds gently through the city, dividing it into two, connected by three bridges — the **Rialto**, the **Scalzi** and the **Accademia**.

Once upon a time the Grand Canal was the port of Venice, the point of arrival of trade for the flourishing Most Serene Republic. As time went by, the port gradually shifted and the Grand Canal became the « parlor » of Venice, a position it still holds today. From the 15th century on, the old houses in Byzantine style which lined the canal were replaced by prestigious palaces built along Gothic, Renaissance, or Baroque lines. These were golden centuries for Venice and this was also when various monumental churches went up along the Grand Canal, punctuating the procession of noble palaces. Churches such as the **Church of San Simeon Piccolo**, the **Church of the Scalzi**, with its monumental Baroque facade; the imposing **Church of San Geremia**, rebuilt in the 18th century; the 17th-century **Church of San Stae**, the **Church of San Samuele** dating back to the 11th century but rebuilt at the end of the 17th; the mighty **Church of Santa Maria della Salute**, one of the most interesting examples of Baroque architecture in Venice. But of equal interest from an architectural and stylistic point of view are the 17th-century **Palazzo Flangini**, the **Palazzo Querini** with its Gothic-Byzantine layout; the 17th-century **Palazzo Correr Contarini**, the 15th-century **Palazzo Giovanelli** with its striking Gothic structure, the elegant **Palazzo Vendramin-Calergi**, one of the finest Renaissance buildings in Venice and famous above all as the seat of the **Casinò Municipale**. Not to be overlooked are the unusual **Palazzo Belloni Battaglia** built in the same years as the Church of Santa Maria della Salute by the great architect Baldassarre Longhena; the spectacular scenographic **Fondaco dei Turchi** with its Venetian-Byzantine characteristics dating to the 12th and 13th centuries, seat of the **Museum of Natural History**; the **Ca' Corner della Regina** in 18th-century style, headquarters for the **Venice Biennale**; the **Ca' Pesaro**, remarkable example of Venetian Baroque and seat of the **Museums of Modern Art** and of **Oriental Art**; the sensual **Palazzo Sagreto**, Byzantine in origin but remodelled in the Gothic period; the 15th-century **Ca' d'Oro** with its ornate facade, housing the **Franchetti Gallery**. Next follows the **Fondaco dei Tedeschi**, an unusual example of 13th-century architecture, with the **Palazzo dei Camarlinghi** built in the 16th century along sober elegant lines; the **Palazzo Grimani**, one of the most interesting 16th-century buildings, and the sumptuous **Palazzo Papadopoli**, to continue with the 18th-century **Palazzo Grassi**, the **Palazzo Contarini degli Scrigni**, a fusion of two buildings of different periods (Renaissance, the one, Baroque the other), with the imposing **Palazzo Corner della Ca' Granda** built in the 16th century after plans by Sansovino and now housing the Prefettura. On the final stretch note should be taken of the exceptional **Palazzo Dario**, the most original example of 16th-century Venetian architecture, the **Palazzo Venier dei Leoni** with the **Peggy Guggenheim Collection**, and finally the **Doges' Palace**, rebuilt in the 12th century on 9th century foundations and then frequently restructured and enlarged in the ensuing centuries.

A view of the Grand Canal.

AN SIMEON PICCOLO

ne Church of San Simeon Piccolo overlooks the Grand anal and almost reaches up to the edge of the water with e spacious entrance staircase. The building next to it is an ample of mature 16th-century architecture, and housed e Scuola dei Tessitori di Panni di Lana (School for Woolen loth Weavers) whose patron saint was St. Simon.

ne original church, dedicated like this one, to the apostles . Simon and St. Jude, was built in the 9th century. In 1718 was torn down and replaced by the new church designed y Giovanni Scalfarotto on ideas by Longhena. Completed 1738 the exterior is characterized by the greenish dome, eathed in copper, with the figure of the *Redeemer* on top the columned lantern. It is said that when Napoleon saw e building he remarked: « I have seen churches without omes, but never a dome without a church ». Apart from apoleon's joking remark, the church really does look too nall under the large dome, preceded by the spacious stair-ase and the tetrastyle porch which reduce the mass of the cade. The relief depicting the *Martyrdom of St. Simon and . Jude* in the elegant pediment above the Corinthian olumns is by Cabianca.

ne **interior** with its circular ground plan is decorated with ilaster strips and columns, between which four altars open ff. These are enriched by various works, as for instance *aint Simon, Jude and John the Baptist* by Polazzo. Statues the Apostles are in the apse near the high altar, which is ecorated with 18th-century statues of *St. Simon and St. latthew*. Of note also the marble *Crucifix* by Marchiari in e **Sacristy**.

terior of the church of San Simeon Piccolo, characterized by great copper-green dome.

lazzo Foscari-Contarini, dating to the first half of the 16th ntury.

FROM THE PONTE DEGLI SCALZI TO THE PONTE DI RIALTO

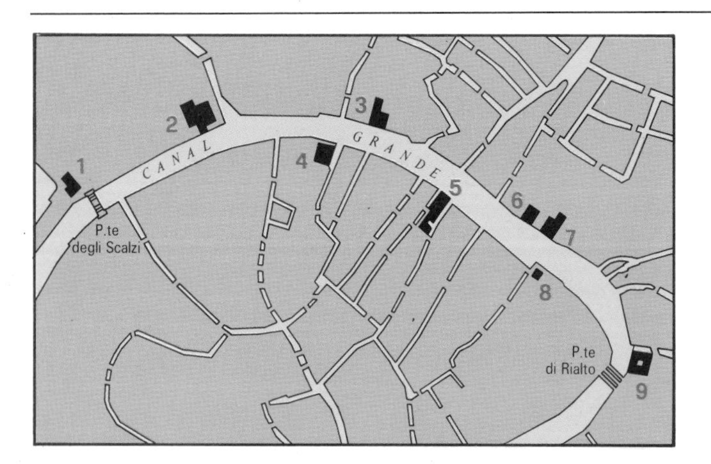

1 - Church of the Scalzi
2 - Church of San Geremia
3 - Palazzo Vendramin Calergi
4 - Fondaco dei Turchi
5 - Ca' Pesaro
6 - Ca' d'Oro
7 - Palazzo Sagredo
8 - Pescaria
9 - Fondaco dei Tedeschi

CHURCH OF THE SCALZI

It took 35 years to finish the Church of the Scalzi or of Santa Maria di Nazareth, begun in 1670, and commissioned from Baldassarre Longhena by the Barefooted Carmelite Fathers for whom a convent and a small church dedicated to Santa Maria di Nazareth had previously been built. The facade by G. Sardi successfully combines the Venetian Baroque with classic forms. During World War I a fresco by Tiepolo, representing the *Transportation of the House of Loreto*, was destroyed. It has been replaced by a painting of the *Proclamation of the Maternity of the Virgin at the Council of Ephesus*, by Ettore Tito.

The **interior** has three chapels on either side of the nav The vault of the chapel on the right was painted by Tiepol who also decorated the first chapel on the left. Ludovic Manin, the last doge of the Serenissima, is buried in th church.

CHURCH OF SAN GEREMIA

San Geremia, near the Palazzo Labia, was restructured i the 18th century on the old 13th-century church. The fir Romanesque campanile in brick, one of the oldest in th city, dates to the 1200s.

he Ponte degli Scalzi, built in stone
1934 to replace the 19th-century
ridge in iron.

he church of San Geremia.

anta Maria di Nazareth known also
s the church of the Scalzi when
e Barefooted Carmelite Fathers took
as their headquarters.

PALAZZO VENDRAMIN-CALERGI

The loveliest palace in Lombardesque style is unquestionably the Palazzo Vendramin-Calergi at the Maddalena. Built between 1504 and 1509 by the Lombardos on designs by Mauro Codussi, two floors of loggias with large arches and two-light openings characterize the large finely proportioned facade. In the 17th century a wing with garden, designed by the architect Scamozzi, was added, only to be torn down later and then rebuilt from scratch. It was in this palace that Richard Wagner died in 1883.

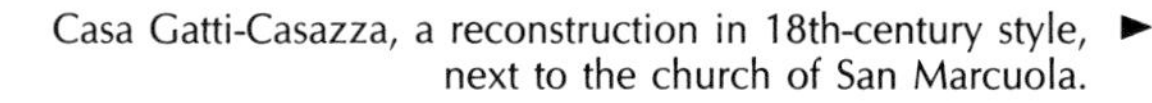

Casa Gatti-Casazza, a reconstruction in 18th-century style, next to the church of San Marcuola. ►

The Renaissance facade of the Palazzo Vendramin-Calergi, seat of the Casino Municipale. ►

The church of San Marcuola serves as backdrop for the Campo dei SS. Ermagora e Fortunato. The facade is incomplete but preserves the portal of the original 18th-century project by Giorgio Massari. Actually tradition sets the foundation of the church in the 9th century. Remodelled in the 17th century, it was definitively transformed by Gaspari, but he had not yet terminated work in 1728 and it was carried out by Massari in 1736, except for the facade.

FONDACO DEI TURCHI

The Fondaco dei Turchi is one of the first warehouses to have been founded in Venice. The basic layout, in fact dates to the 12th-13th centuries, and is Veneto-Byzantine in style. It was acquired in 1381 by the Republic who turned it over to the dukes of Ferrara. It then belonged to various wealthy families and ended up by becoming the warehouse and headquarters of the Turkish community between 162 and 1838. It was originally of such beauty that the Serenissima used it as a guest house for important personages. Even so the exterior is now quite different from what it looked like originally: between 1858 and 1869 Berchet restored it completely altering the structures and the facade.

CA' PESARO

The Palazzo Pesaro is by Baldassarre Longhena, one of the greatest architects of the 17th century. It was begun in 165. and finished by Antonio Gaspari. The facade is decorated with masks and various ornaments with busts of animals.

The Fondaco dei Turchi, one of whose illustrious guests was the emperor of Constantinople. It is now the seat of the Museum of Natural History.

Ca' Pesaro with the Rio di Naole in the background.

Palazzo di Ca' Pesaro, seat of the Museum of Modern Art

Palazzo Gussoni, subsequently Gussoni Grimani "della Vida" dates to the 16th century, perhaps on designs by Sanmicheli. Unfortunately all the exterior decoration by Tintoretto has been lost

CA' PESARO
MUSEO
D'ARTE MODERNA

CA' D'ORO

The famous Ca' d'Oro, far and away the finest example o flamboyant Gothic, houses the **Franchetti Gallery**. Th palace was built for Marino Contarini between 1424 an 1430 by Giovanni and Bartolomeo Bon. The name derive from the marble tracery and the gilding which once decora ed the facade. In 1846 Giovanni Battista Meduna bega restoration but removed and sold the original facing, fo which he was brought to court. After changing hands man times, the palace finally came into the possession of Baro Giorgio Franchetti who restored it completely before dona ing the palace and the works it contained to the city i 1915. The ashes of the baron repose under a column in th palace courtyard.

The Ca' d'Oro is the most perfect example of flamboyant Gothic architecture in Venice: below, a detail of the facade.

A fine picture of the palaces that border the left bank of th Grand Canal. To the left of the Ca' d'Oro, the Palazzo Mia Coletti Giusti and the 17th-century Palazzo Fonta Rezzonico. To the right of the Ca' d'Oro is the Palazz Pesar

Palazzo Pesaro, in 15th-century Venetian Gothic style, wi the adjacent facade of Palazzo Morosini-Sagredo. The latt originally dates to the Byzantine period (13th cent.) but it w remodelled in later centurie

PALAZZO SAGREDO

The late 14th-century Palazzo Sagredo — now Istituto Ra — is near the Ca' d'Oro. There is an elegant four-light ope ing on the upper floor surrounded by a Venetian-Byzanti frieze, and a fine six-light opening on the lower floor.

The Grand Canal with some of its palaces: Michiel de Colonne, Michiel dal Brusà and Smith Mangilli Valmarar which also look out on the Rio dei SS. Aposto

Rio delle Beccarie and the Pescar

Still another picture of the lovely Palazzo Sagredo.

Campo di Santa Sofia and the small Palazzo Foscari del Prà, erected in the second half of the 15th century. The ambassador of Mantua lived here in 1520.

PESCARIA

The statue of *St. Peter* decorates the arcading of the Pescaria on the side which overlooks the Grand Canal. The neo-Gothic forms were designed in 1907 by Rupolo and Laurenti, who skillfully harmonized them with the neighboring structures. This was once the site of the 13th-century house of the Querini who took part in the conspiracy of Bajamont Tiepolo and who then had their house confiscated and almost totally destroyed, with the exception of a few arches and a two-light opening towards the Campo delle Beccarie. This large portico is now the headquarters of the fish market, facing out on the Grand Canal and the Rio delle Beccarie to facilitate restocking, not far from the Cordaria, the Erbaria and the Casaria, where fruit and cheese are sold.

picture of the Pescaria and, in the photo below, a panorama Venetian palaces: Palazzo Michiel delle Colonne, Palazzo chiel de Brusa and Palazzo Mangilli-Valmarana. The name the second palace clearly refers to the fire (brusa = scorch burn) which gutted it in 1774. The last-named palace was abode of the English consul Joseph Smith, a passionate lector of art and patron of artists including Rosalba Carriera, Ricci and above all Canaletto. His collection included out 50 canvases and over 140 drawings by Canaletto and in 60 he left them all to the English Crown.

FONDACO DEI TEDESCHI

Next to the eastern end of the Ponte di Rialto is the Fonda (or in Venetian dialect, Fontego) dei Tedeschi, a magni cent early 16th-century building. This large warehouse a clustering of shops already existed in the 13th century, b it was wiped out by a fire and then rebuilt in its prese forms. Even so the facade on the Grand Canal is no long just as Girolamo Tedesco designed it, for the two towers the corners were demolished in the 19th century. The ori nal structure, built by the architects Spavento and Scarpa nino between 1505 and 1508 had also been covered wi magnificent frescoes by Giorgione and Titian, which co tinued around the side overlooking the Salizzada del Fon go. Time has cancelled almost all traces, except for a fe fragments now in the Accademia.

The imposing headquarters for the German merchants Venice — a particularly numerous colony which played important role in the economy of the city — has a spacio internal courtyard, surrounded by loggias, once open b now closed by a skylight which lets light into the form merchant warehouse, now the post office.

Palazzo Ca' da Mosto, built between the 11th and 13th century. From the 16th to the 18th century the palace became the "Albergo del Leon Bianco", one of the best and most important hotels in Venice.

The twenty-five arches of the Fabbriche Nuove di Rialto, possibly built on designs by Jacopo Sansovino between 1552 and 1555.

ne Fondaco dei Tedeschi.

On the following pages: the Ponte di Rialto.

COMUNE DI VENEZIA ASSESSORATO
L'ARTE DEL M
PRIMA DI CO
PRESENTATA DA OLIVE
PALAZZO DUCALE 12 GIUGNO- 23 OTTOBRE -APERTO TUT

Two pictures of the famous Ponte di Rialto: the cost of rebuilding it in stone, on a project by Antonio da Ponte, cost all of 250,000 ducats in 1590. The single span is notched into the fondamenta.

PONTE DI RIALTO

The first Rialto Bridge was called « della Moneta ». The original pontoon bridge was erected by Nicolo Barattieri and the wooden structure which replaced it was destroyed during the uprisings in the plot of Bajamonte Tiepolo. The next bridge collapsed in 1444 and was replaced by one which included a drawbridge and shops. When this also showed signs of instability, it was rebuilt in stone, preference being given to the design by Antonio Ponte, rather than to those of famous architects such as Michelangelo, Sansovino, and Palladio.

The bridge (finished in 1592) has a single span of 28 meter (at the point where the Grand Canal is narrowest) and is 7. meters above the water-line.

HE HISTORICAL REGATTA

)ne of the festivals in Venice which is still in full force is ıe Historical Regatta, providing entertainment for the 'enetians and all those who come from near and far to see ıe colorful event. Many doubts exist as to when the first egatta was held and why, but we do know that in the 13th-4th centuries the race had become customary. As is still ıe case today, the race itself was preceded by a sumptuous rocession of all kinds of boats, all decked out and bearing ymbolic images. The finest of all was the **Bucintoro**, the oge's ceremonial barge, now replaced by a smaller ver-ion. An idea of what the original gilded galley looked like provided by various paintings and the model in the Naval Auseum. After the parade, which was once a real *défilé* for ıe nobility, the races began. Originally the boats were ivided into categories according to the number of rowers nce even twenty or fifty), but now there are only two per oat. The route to be covered in the least possible time goes om the Motta to Castello and Santa Chiara on the Grand Canal and back to the Ca' Foscari where a floating pavilion *nachina*) marks the finish line. The winning team is award-d with a banner while a piglet is jokingly « conferred » on ıe loser.

shot of the famous Historical Regatta.

hree views of the lively Ponte di Rialto and a detail of the abernacle with the Virgin set into the side of the arch.

)n the following pages: the Regatta in the Canal Grande, chool of Canaletto (Museo Correr).

FROM THE PONTE DI RIALTO TO SAN MARCO

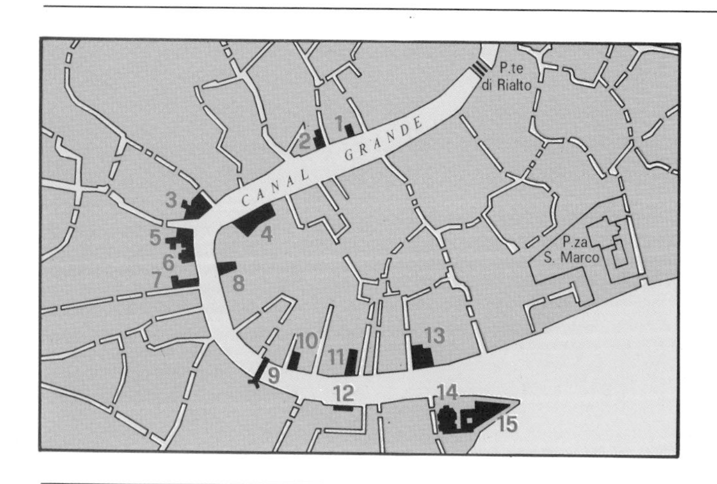

1 - Palazzo Papadopoli
2 - Palazzo Bernardo
3 - Palazzo Balbi
4 - Palazzo Nani-Mocenigo
5 - Ca' Foscari
6 - Palazzo Giustinian
7 - Ca' Rezzonico
8 - Palazzo Grassi
9 - Ponte dell'Accademia
10 - Palazzo Barbaro
11 - Ca' Granda
12 - Collection Guggenheim
13 - Palazzo Contarini Fasan
14 - Church of Santa Maria della Salute
15 - Dogana da Mar

The Ponte di Rialto seen from the Riva del Vin.

ALAZZO PAPADOPOLI

ne Renaissance Palazzo Papadopoli is a two-story building tributed to Gian Giacomo dei Grigi. Of particular note the ne cornice with small oval windows and two obelisks bove. Inside are to be found paintings by Tiepolo and etro Longhi.

ALAZZO BERNARDO

alazzo Bernardo must be cited as one of the best examples Gothic style, both on account of its sumptuous ornament nd the harmonious forms, where voids and solids are perctly balanced. Built in 1442, there are two six-light winows on the first two floors, each surmounted by a four-light pening; of note in the courtyard is a fine open staircase.

A picture of the Grand Canal with Palazzo Papadopoli, Palazzo Businello (built in the 17th century on a preexisting Byzantine structure) and the contiguous Palazzo Lanfranchi.

A view of the Ponte di Rialto and the Riva del Ferro.

A' FOSCARI

n outstanding example of flamboyant Gothic is Ca' oscari, one of the loveliest buildings in Venice. The facade richly decorated in marble with two superposed loggias eight arches each, surrounded by windows which repeat e decorative motive. The whole is crowned by an imposg motive of arches, with a central four-light opening at the ppermost floor. The palace originally belonged to the iustinian family, was acquired by the Republic, and given st to the Duke of Mantua and then to Francesco Sforza. was auctioned off in 1452 and became the property of oge Foscari.

ALAZZO BALBI

alazzo Balbi, facing onto the canal (« in volta di canal »), uilt at the end of the 16th century after a design by Alesandro Vittoria, in a sense seems to mark the transition beveen the sober spatial proportions of the Renaissance and e heavy decoration of the Baroque.

ALAZZO NANI-MOCENIGO

alazzo Nani-Mocenigo, formerly Erizzo, stands on the left ank of the Grand Canal. Built in the 15th century, it is haracterized by the first- floor windows with dentellated urrounds framing carenate arches.

alazzo Giustinian Persico, built in Renaissance style at the eginning of the 16th century, stands at the corner between e Grand Canal and the Rio di San Toma.

hree of the most prestigious Venetian palaces which overlook e Grand Canal: Palazzo Foscari, Palazzo Balbi and Palazzo ani Mocenigo.

PALAZZO GRASSI

This imposing building, by the architect Giorgio Massari, one of the finest examples of 18th-century architecture. (either side of the tall portal, Palazzo Grassi has two tiers windows, set into the rustication, above which are tv other tiers of balconied windows, simple and elegant. now houses the Centro delle Arti e del Costume and is t permanent headquarters for all kinds of cultural activiti

PONTE DELL'ACCADEMIA

The southernmost crossing on the Grand Canal is the A cademia Bridge whose broad wooden span connects Ca po San Vidal to Campo della Carità with the Scuola Granc di Santa Maria della Carità, now the site of the Galleria de l'Accademia.

The origins of this footbridge are not as old as the use wood, typical for the 14th-century Venetian bridges, wou lead one to believe. It is a modern (1934) structure, by M ozzi, and was erected as a temporary replacement for tl metal bridge which had been built in 1854 and was soc criticized as being excessively « modern ». The same thi happened for the Ponte degli Scalzi. Plans were therefo made for a stone bridge, closer in style to the adjacent buil ings, so that the historical Ponte di Rialto would be flank by two other bridges in Istrian stone at the Scalzi and at tl Accademia. Only the former however was actually built

Palazzo Grassi.

The Ponte dell'Accademia and the Palazzo Cavalli Franche where the archduke Frederick of Austria died in 18

at year — 1934 — and a temporary structure went up for e latter. Eventually this was accepted as definitive, despite e fact that today the material of which it is made clearly etrays the passage of time.

ALAZZI GIUSTINIAN

arious palaces go by the name of the powerful Giustinian mily, from the one at the Traghetto di Calle Vellaresso, ating to 1474 — headquarters of the offices of the Biennale to the one near Ca' Foscari which consists of twin buildgs with loggias of quadrilobate arches and was where 'agner also lived.

A' REZZONICO

alazzo Rezzonico was begun by Longhena and terminated 1745 by Giorgio Massari. It is a typical example of 18th-entury architecture and quite suitably houses the Museum f the Eighteenth Century (Museo del Settecento). The uilding stretches out along the Grand Canal and the faade, enlivened by balconies, is ornamented with columns nd sculpture.

Palazzo Giustinian Lolin, an early work by Baldassarre Longhena, with the two pinnacles decorating the roof, and the 16th-century Palazzo Civran Badoer Barozzi.

Ca' Rezzonico.

PALAZZO BARBARO

Near the Ponte dell'Accademia, on the left of the Grand Canal is the Palazzo Barbaro (15th cent.) with four-light windows with carenate arches on the upper floors and a fine Renaissance portal with medallions of the emperors.

SCUOLA GRANDE DI SANTA MARIA DELLA CARITÀ

The Scuola Grande di Santa Maria della Carità was founded in 1260 at San Leonardo but was then transferred, first to the Oratory of San Giacomo Apostolo, and then to an Oratory of its own near the Church of Santa Maria della Carità. A *Madonna with Confraternity Brothers* is set over the portal with the Confraternity patron saints, *Christopher and Leonardo*, on either side. The large room on the ground floor is divided into two parts, one serving as entrance to the **Gallerie dell'Accademia** and the other as the hall of the **Accademia delle Belle Arti**. Works originally in the guest-room include a reliquary donated in 1463 by Cardinal Bessarione, the *Presentation of the Virgin*, painted for the Confraternity by Titian, and the large *Triptych* by Antonio Vivarini and Giovanni d'Alemagna of the *Virgin and Child with the Doctors of the Church*, as well as works by Bellini, C Mansueti, G. Cignaroli, J. Guarana, G. D. Tiepolo, an Marieschi.

CA' GRANDA

Palazzo Corner, known as Ca' Granda, is one of the mo imposing examples of Renaissance architecture. By Jacop Sansovino (1537), it is the seat of the Prefecture. The facad is divided into three stories — rusticated, Ionic and Corir thian, with three arches on the ground floor and larg round-headed arches on the windows. Of note, inside, majestic courtyard with a statue of *Apollo* by Cabianca.

The Grand Canal with, left to right, the Palazzo Cavalli Franchetti and the Palazzo Barbaro now Curtis, separated by the Rio dell'Orso. In the background on the right, the church of Santa Maria della Salute.

Above: on the left the Palazzo Brandolini Rota (in which th poet Robert Browning lived in 1878) and the back of th Ponte dell'Accademia; on the right the front view of th Galleria dell'Accademia (Giogio Massari and Bernardin Maccarucci, 1756-65). Below: on the left the Palazzo Corner dell Ca' Granda, so-called for its majestic proportions; on the righ the Palazzo Minotto, originally Byzantine and rebuilt i Gothic style during the 15th century

ACCADEMIA
DI BELLE ARTI
PAOLO VERONESE

A view of Palazzo Barbaro (left) and Palazzo Dario (right). The first was built in Gothic style in the middle of the 15th century. The second with its strongly tilted silhouette, was built in 1478 for Giovanni Dario, secretary of the Republic in Constantinople. The originally Gothic building has a Renaissance facade by Pietro Lombardo, characterized by polychrome marble inlays which form medallions and plates.

Palazzo Venier dei Leoni: the building which overlooks the Grand Canal is only the ground floor of what, as initially planned, was to have been a palace as imposing as the Corner della Ca' Granda across the way. The palace, begun in 1749 by Boschetti but never finished for lack of funds, owes its name to the fact that noble Venier family used to keep one or more lions in the garden. It was bought by the famous American art collector Peggy Guggenheim, and today is the seat of one the most prestigious collections of contemporary art: from Bacon to Picasso, from Braque to Kandinsky, from Ernst to Dali, etc.

GUGGENHEIM COLLECTION

The most important Italian collection of contemporary art is without the shadow of a doubt the Guggenheim Collection, housed in the **Palazzo Venir dei Leoni** on the Grand Canal, a building begun in 1749 on designs by Lorenzo Boschetti. It was never completed and is surrounded by a fine garden. The works of art on exhibit furnish a complete picture of the avant-garde artistic movements of the 20th century, from Cubism, with paintings by Picasso — *The Poet, Lacerba* —, Duchamp — *Sad Young Man in a Train* —, Bracque, Kupka, Marcoussis, to Futurism with works by Boccioni, E. Prampolini, G. Severini. Abstract art is represented by Kandinsky, Mondrian — *The Sea* —, Malevich — with *Suprematist Composition*, while particular attention is paid to Dadaism and Surrealism (particularly in view of the ties between Peggy Guggenheim and Max Ernst, a painter whose place in the historical avant-garde is ensured), with works by De Chi co, Ernst — of his many paintings mention is made of *T Kiss, The Forest, Zoomorphic Couple* —, Magritte, Pa Klee, Picabia and Mirò.
The collection includes examples of the more recent ava garde movements as well, both European and America with works by Moore, Pollock and Arnaldo Pomodoro.

Palazzo Barbarigo, 16th century, stands at the corner betwe the Grand Canal and the Campo San Lio: the mosaics t decorate the facade in parallel bands are 19th-century a were taken from cartoons by Giulio Carl

A picture of the Grand Canal with a gondola — the clas Venetian boat — and, on the right, the Palazzo Pisani Gri

BIENNALE DI VENEZIA

Above, left to right: the Palazzo Contarini Fasan with its lovely balusters in openwork marble on the terraces and the Palazzo Contarini in Gothic style and dating to the 15th century. Below: the last stretch of the Grand Canal in the vicinity of the Piazzetta San Marco. On the left is the Palazzo Giustinian – a 15th-century building — at present headquarters for the offices of the Biennale, and a series of unimposing buildings.

The domes of the church of Santa Maria della Salute and the Punta della Dogana.

PALAZZO CONTARINI-FASAN

The delightful small Contarini-Fasan palace, built around 1475 and popularly known as the « house of Desdemona », stands on the left bank of the Grand Canal, near the Rio delle Ostreghe, and is decorated with charming tracery balconies.

CHURCH OF SANTA MARIA DELLA SALUTE

In 1630 with the plague raging in Venice, the Senate made a vow to erect a church to the Madonna when the scourge came to an end. In fulfillment of this obligation Baldassarre Longhena designed Santa Maria della Salute, which was consecrated in 1687, five years after the architect's death. The church is unquestionably one of the great monuments of the Venetian Baroque.

The building is octagonal in plan with arches dominated by a dome on a drum and with six side chapels. A flight of stairs leads to the **facade** which looks like a rich triumphal arch, with chapels set into the sides of the octagon. The first three altars on the right in the **interior** have paintings by Luca Giordano and the third altar on the left has a late work by Titian of the *Pentecost*. Around 1674 Giusto Le Court created the marble group on the high altar, meant to house the Holy Image that was venerated in San Tito in Candia and then brought to Venice in 1672 when the Turks occupied the city. The sculpture shows us the *Plague fleeing from the Madonna*. Originally the commission was to have been given to Bernini, but he refused. Canvases by Titian are in the ceiling of the large Sacristy and the tabernacle has a fine mosaic in pietra dure of the Byzantine school of the 12th century. The Venetians flock to the church in pilgrimage on the 21st of November, the day dedicated to the Madonna della Salute.

e Palazzo Genovese, of 1892, and the church of the Salute.

Aerial view of the Punta della Dogana dominated by the church of Santa Maria della Salute.

OGANA DA MAR

e complex of the Maritime Customs House, at the far end the sestiere (district) of Dorsoduro, is a sort of spearhead tting out into the lagoon and dividing the Grand Canal m the Canal of the Giudecca. Behind it, beyond the minary, Santa Maria della Salute looms up.
the beginning of the 15th century, the area whose ele- nt layout we now admire was already used for the dock- g of ships from the Orient and their clearance by customs. e sheds built to house the merchandise and the customs icials were rebuilt more than once. The construction of the **Punta della Dogana** with a tower which rises up over the terraced porch dates to 1677. Set on a base on the roof of the tower are figures of two slaves holding up a large gilded sphere on which the statue of *Fortune* (a 17th-century work by Giuseppe Bononi) stands on one foot, free to turn with the wind, as changeable as human destinies at the mercy of the seas and trade.
The arcaded structures along the sides date, as can be seen, to different periods. Parts are in stone with light-colored arched openings and parts are completely faced in white on more serried rows of arches. The latest renovation was carried out by Pigazzi, in 1838.

SESTIERI OF CANNAREGIO, SAN MARCO, CASTELLO

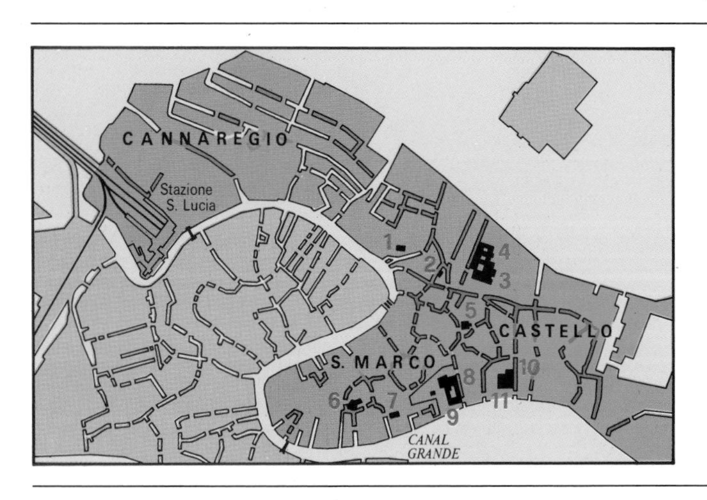

1 - Church of Santi Apostoli
2 - Church of Santa Maria dei Miracoli
3 - Church of Santi Giovanni e Paolo
4 - Scuola Grande di San Marco
5 - Church of Santa Maria Formosa
6 - Gran Teatro La Fenice
7 - Church of San Moisè
8 - San Marco
9 - Palace of the Doges
10 - Church of San Zaccaria

CHURCH OF THE SANTI APOSTOLI

The extremely old church of the Santi Apostoli was frequently remodelled up to 1575 when it was radically renovated. In the 18th century Giuseppe Pedola once more changed its form. The **facade** is in brick. **Inside** — a single rectangular nave — the **Corner Chapel** contains the *Tomb of Marco Corner,* attributed to Tulio Lombardo. The altarpiece with the *Communion of St. Lucy* is by G. B. Tiepolo.

The church of the Santi Apostoli.

CHURCH OF SANTA MARIA DEI MIRACOLI

In 1481 Pietro Lombardo began the construction of Sar Maria dei Miracoli in Lombard style. The **facade** with marble facing in two tiers is particularly striking. Two lar windows are set above the central portal. The walls of t single-nave **interior** are faced with fine marble and t barrel-vaulted ceiling is decorated with coffering containi the heads of *Prophets and Saints* by Pier Maria Pennacc

The original facade of the church of Santa Maria dei Miracoli.

he sanctuary has an elegant staircase with statues of *St. rancis, St. Claire*, the *Virgin of the Annunciation and iabriel*, by Tullio Lombardo. The high altar is crowned by dome.

EATRO LA FENICE

he monumental entrance to the Gran Teatro La Fenice, the nost famous of the Venetian theaters which survived the risis that marked the death knell for many of the city stages, pens off Campo San Fantini. It was decided to build La enice despite the fact that a law prohibited the construction of new theaters. After special permission had been obained, the announcement of the competition for the project vas published on November 1, 1789. Twenty-nine roposals were entered and the winner was G. A. Selva, vho succeeded in completing the theater in 27 months, of vhich only 18 were devoted to the construction. The entire ost of 408,377 ducats was paid for by the owners of the oxes. It was inaugurated on May 16, 1792, during the Festa della Sensa with the drama *I Giuochi di Agrigento* by Count Alessandro Pepoli, music by Giovanni Paisiello. Apart from the ever-present financial problems, the theater vas an immediate enormous success.
The night between the 12th and the 13th of December, 1836, a fire destroyed a large part of the structure, which vas restored by Tommaso and Giovanbattista Meduna. In he brief period of the Republic of Daniele Manin, only conerts to collect funds for the resistance against the Austrians vere given. After Villafranca it was decided to keep the

xterior and interior of the famous Teatro La Fenice.

The 17th-century facade of the church of San Moisè.

theater closed until better times and not even the insistency of the Imperial Regia Lieutenancy succeeded in reversing this decision. By contrast, the season which followed the annexation to Italy was truly extraordinary. Giuseppe Verdi's *Un Ballo in Maschera* and Vincenzo Bellini's *Norma* were both on the bill. On November 8, 1866, the Venetians flocked to the Teatro La Fenice to render homage to Victor Emmanuel II for whom the cantata « *Venezia al Re* » was played.
In 1938, after being partly restructured, La Fenice became an Autonomous Organization and was newly decorated by the painter Giuseppe Cherubini.
The **exterior** of the building is now in a neoclassical style, with a columned porch set under niches containing statues of *Music* and the *Dance* (by Meduna), and decorated with masks and a medallion with the *Phoenix*. **Inside**, the vast orchestra is surrounded by the gallery and four tiers of boxes (balustrades richly ornamented with gilded reliefs and painted medallions) with a seating capacity of about 1500.

CHURCH OF SAN MOISÈ

The original 8th-century church was rebuilt in the 10th century for a certain Moisè Venier who wanted it dedicated to his patron saint. In the 14th century a campanile in brick with two-light openings in the belfry was added. The facade, which is particularly lovely, with a wealth of sculpture, is the work of Alessandro Tremignon and the sculptor Enrico Meyring and dates to the second half of the 17th century.
The church with its single nave contains many 17th- an 18th-century paintings. Carved wooden *choir stalls* datin to the 16th century are in the sanctuary. In the chapel o the left are a *Last Supper* by Palma Giovane and a *Washin of the Feet* by Jacopo Tintoretto.

CHURCH OF SAN ZACCARIA

The original Church of San Zaccaria dates to the 9th centur but it was rebuilt after the fire of 1105 and transformed i Gothic style between the 15th and 16th centuries by Antc nio Gambello and Mauro Codussi. The extremely tall **fa cade** has a large arched pediment as its crowning elemer with a row of blind niches and decorative panels. The love ly statue of *St. Zaccariah* over the portal is by Alessandr Vittoria.
The **interior** (with tall columns dividing the two side aisle from the nave in a perfect fusion of Gothic and Renaissanc styles) contains an *altarpiece* by Giovanni Bellini, a *Mador na and Saints* by Palma Vecchio, the *Birth of the Baptist* b Tintoretto and the *Flight to Egypt* by G. D. Tiepolo. *Frescoe* by Andrea del Castagno are to be seen in the **San Tarasi Chapel**, as well as three *polyptychs* by Giovanni d'Alema gna and Antonio Vivarini. The sepulcher of A. Vittorio, wit his self-portrait, is at the back of the left aisle. The two hol water fonts in the church as well as the statues of the *Baptis* and of *St. Zaccariah* near the entrance are by Vittoria. In hi testament he also donated his house in Calle della Pietà t the nuns of San Zaccaria and asked to be buried in th church.

The facade of the church of San Zaccaria.

n Zaccaria, interior: the famous altarpiece by Bellini.

CHURCH OF SANTI GIOVANNI E PAOLO (SAN ZANIPOLO)

The construction of the church of Santi Giovanni e Paolo or San Zanipolo was begun in 1246, but it was not till 200 years later, in 1430, that the building could be termed finished. It is, without doubt, a stupendous example of Venetian Gothic. The church was used for the funerals of the doges and every year, on June 26th, was visited by the doge and the high officials.
The mortal remains of various doges and condottieri lie with-in the church, including Jacopo and Lorenzo Tiepolo, Daniele Boni. Nor should one overlook the *Mausoleum to the Valier Family* by Andrea Tirali, the various *monuments of the Mocenigo and Valier families*, as well as the *Monument to Bartolomeo Bragadin* in Lombardesque style and the one to *Marcantonio Bragadin* by Scamozzi. And then the *Tomb of Vettor Pisani*, the *Monument to Doge Marco Corner*, in Gothic style.
Artists such as Giovanni Bellini, Piazzetta, Lorenzo Lotto, B. Vivarini, Palma Giovane and Nino Pisano worked in the church.
Next door is the **Scuola Grande di San Marco**, originally dating to 1260 but then rebuilt after a fire by Pietro Lombardo and Mauro Codussi between 1485 and 1495.

EQUESTRIAN MONUMENT TO BARTOLOMEO COLLEONI

The equestrian statue of Bartolomeo Colleoni looms up on a high pedestal in the Campo dei Santi Giovanni e Paolo, in front of the Scuola Grande di San Marco. This mercenary captain was involved in various exploits on the side of th Serenissima in the war against Filippo Maria Visconti 1431, helping to counterbalance the negative trend of th campaigns undertaken by Carmagnola. When hostiliti with the Visconti were resumed, Colleoni — together wi Gattamelata — was once more in the ranks of the Venetia (1437-41). After a period passed in the hire of the adve saries, in 1448 he returned to the Serenissima together wi Sforza, responsible for the victories of Caravaggio, Scies Borgomanero and the campaigns in the countryside arour Brescia, Bergamo and Parma. After having passed to th other side for the last time, he finally became head of th Venetian troops from 1454 to 1457, the year of his dea which found him in the pomp of his castle in Malpaga. When he died he left most of his considerable patrimony t the Republic, on the condition that a statue to him be erec ed in Piazza San Marco. Since by law no monument coul be raised there, his statue was placed in Campo Sa Zanipolo.
Andrea Verrocchio worked on the statue between 1481 an 1488 but died before casting it in bronze, a job whic together with the finishing touches, was entrusted to Ale sandro Leopardi, who inaugurated the statue in 1496 aft also having designed the high base with columns an panels.

Aerial view of the church of Santi Giovanni e Paolo.

The church of Santi Giovanni e Paolo, the monument Colleoni and the Scuola Grande di San Marc

CUOLA GRANDE DI SAN MARCO

e phenomenon of the institution in Venice of the called schools was quite complex, for they involved terests of religious, political, social and artistic na-re.

at tendency towards the formation of associations which aracterized the Italian Middle Ages was also evident in nice with congregations and associations whose prime rpose was mutual assistence and works of charity.

cuole » or « Schools » were thus constituted, of greater or sser importance depending on the number of brethren in-lved.

e six Schools known as « Grandi » were solely devotional character.

e Scuola Grande di San Marco founded in 1260 was ce in the edifice which now houses the Ospedale Civile Hospital. Destroyed by fire, it was rebuilt by Mauro dussi and Pietro Lombardo between 1485 and 1495.

e **facade** is a fine example of Renaissance architec-re.

e statues are by B. Bon and Tullio Lombardo. On the first or the **Chapter Hall** has a 16th-century wooden *ceiling* d an *altar* by the school of Sansovino. In the Hostel Hall **ala dell'Albergo**) there is another lovely ceiling with deco-tions in gold and blue, by Pietro and Biagio Faenza. On e walls are paintings by Palma Giovane, Mansueti and ttore Belliniano. The hall also contains the **Medical brary**. The cycle with the *Stories of Saint Mark*, by Carpac-o, the Bellinis, and Tintoretto, some of which are now in e Gallerie dell'Accademia, were originally on the floor ove.

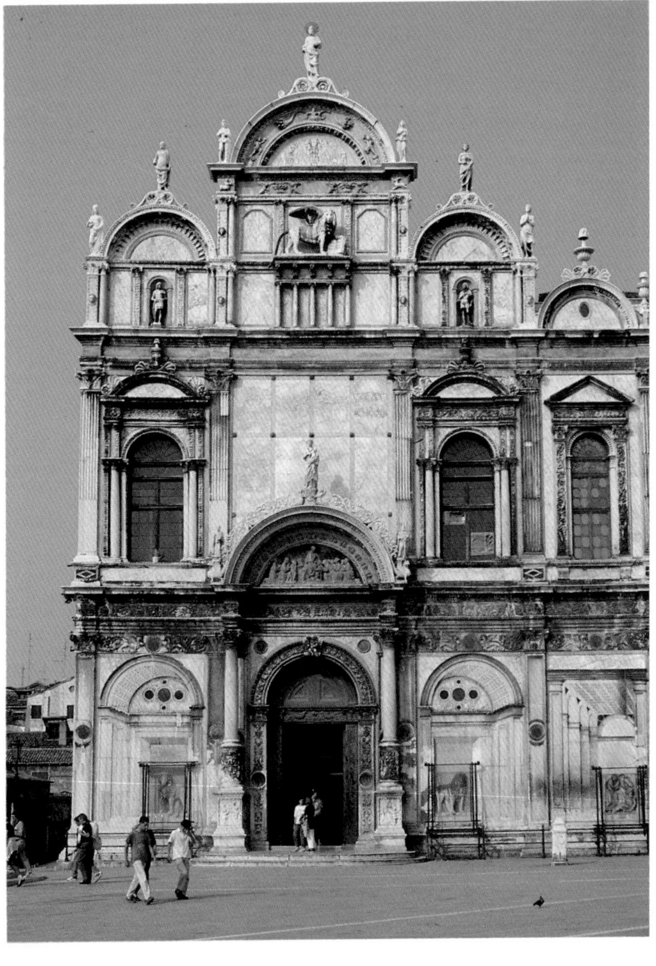

CHURCH OF SANTA MARIA FORMOSA

The original church of Santa Maria Formosa which seems t have been built in the 7th century was renovated time an time again. The present edifice is by Codussi. The two **fa cades** date to different periods (the one facing the bridge t 1541 and the one on the Campo to 1604). The **bell towe** is Baroque with a double balcony on either side of the bel fry and an interesting grotesque mask over the entranc doorway.
The Latin-cross interior has a nave only. A splendid *triptyc* by Bartolomeo Vivarini is in a chapel on the right, while polyptych with *St. Barbara and Four Saints* by Palma Vec chio is in the right transept. Take note of the *altar of th Scuola dei Bombardieri* which had its home in this churc and in which a small bombard is preserved.

Two views of the characteristic Rio Santa Maria Formosa and picture of the church.

SESTIERI OF SANTA CROCE, SAN POLO, DORSODURO

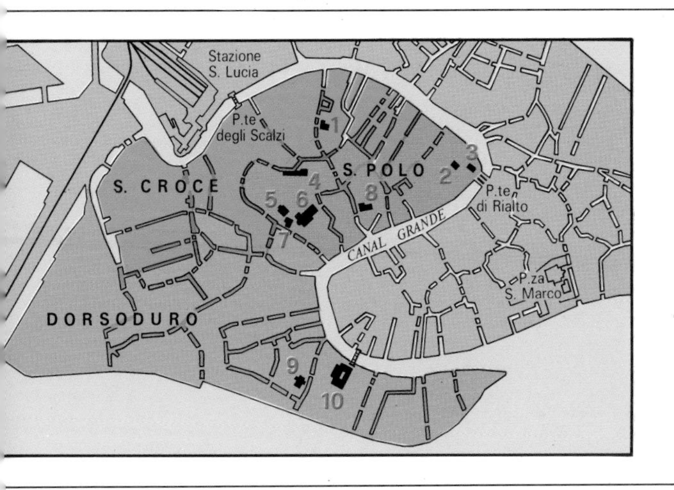

1 - Church of San Giacomo dell'Orio
2 - Church of San Giovanni Elemosinario
3 - Church of San Giacomo di Rialto
4 - Scuola Grande di San Giovanni Evangelista
5 - Church of San Rocco
6 - Church of Santa Maria Gloriosa dei Frari
7 - Scuola Grande di San Rocco
8 - Church of San Polo
9 - Church of San Trovaso
10 - Galleria dell'Accademia

HURCH OF SAN GIACOMO DELL'ORIO

1225 the Church of San Giacomo dell'Orio was rebuilt the site of an earlier 9th-century church and was then novated in the 16th century. To one side is the fine brick **mpanile** with a four-light opening in the belfry. In the tin-cross interior different styles fuse together while a ooden carinate vault covers both sanctuary and crossing. e numerous works of art include an *altarpiece* by ronese, panel paintings by Buonconsiglio and Schiavone, d, in the **Old Sacristy**, a cycle of paintings by Palma Giovne with scenes from the *Old Testament*.

e Fondamenta Papafava and the Ponte Malvasia.

e church of San Giacomo dell'Orio, in the Campo of the ne name and the Rio near the church.

ne distinguished Rio Palazzo.

Ponte Cappello, or dei Garzoti.

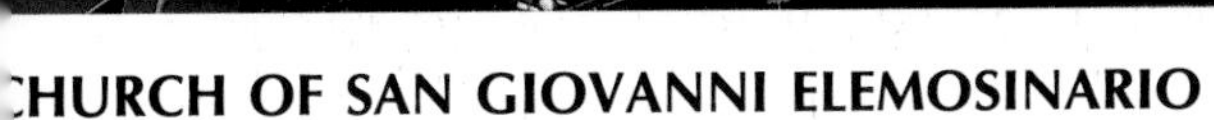
:HURCH OF SAN GIOVANNI ELEMOSINARIO

irst built in the 11th century, San Giovanni Elemosinario vas destroyed by fire in 1513 and rebuilt by Scarpagnino n the same century. It is a Greek cross in plan. The ceiling nd the altar in the sacristy have works by G. B. Pittoni vhile a fine *Saint John Elemosinario* by Titian is on the high ltar in the sanctuary and works by Pordenone and Palma ;iovane are to be found in the side chapels.
)f note the small brick **campanile**, with fine arches in the elfry, which survived the fire of 1513 intact.

:HURCH OF SAN POLO

\pparently San Polo was founded by Doge Pietro Gradeni- jo. It was rebuilt in Gothic style and then frequently emodelled. The brick **campanile** with a conic steeple dates o 1361. The **interior** is a basilica with a nave and two isles. It contains works by Jacopo Tintoretto, Palma Gio- ane, G. B. Tiepolo and Alessandro Vittoria.

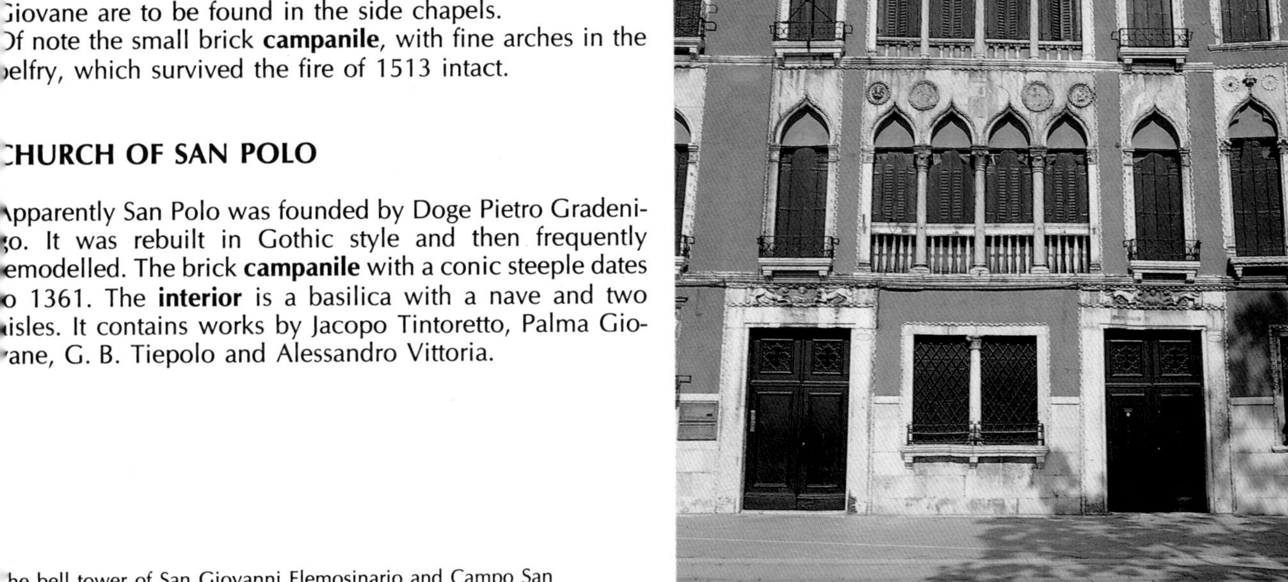

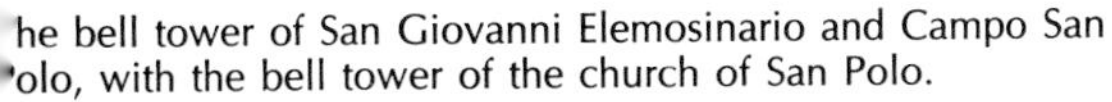
he bell tower of San Giovanni Elemosinario and Campo San 'olo, with the bell tower of the church of San Polo.

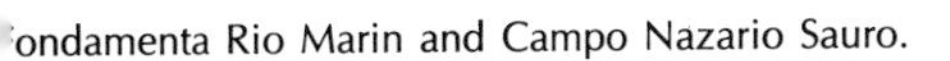
'ondamenta Rio Marin and Campo Nazario Sauro.

SCUOLA GRANDE DI SAN GIOVANNI EVANGELISTA

In 1340, the Confraternity of the Battuti (flagellants), whos patron saint was St. John Evangelist, was housed in th hospice founded in 1261 by the Badoer family. This the became the Scuola Grande di San Giovanni Evangelist. one of the oldest of the Venetian Scuole or Guilds. Th Gothic **facade**, which contains two 14th-century *relie* dates to 1454. In the courtyard of the Scuola note should b taken of the marble Corinthian pilaster strips by Pietro Lon bardo of 1481, and a fine *doorway* built in 1512 after plar by Mauro Codussi. On the ground floor the **interior** has Renaissance hall by Codussi. There is also a hall remodelle by Giorgio Massari in 1727. He also designed the altar, wit an imposing statue of *St. John* by Morlaiter. On the walls a canvases by Longhi and Vicentino while the *ceiling* is dec rated with *scenes from the Apocalypse* by Guarana an Tiepolo. Paintings by Palma Giovane and stucco decor tions are in the **Oratorio della Croce** and the **Sala dei Co vocati**.

CHURCH OF SAN GIACOMO DI RIALTO

The Church of San Giacomo di Rialto, traditionally the o dest church in Venice, is in the Ruga degli Orefici. Datin back to the 11th century, it was completely restored in th 17th century. On the facade over the fine 15th-century po

Rio San Silvestro and a rio in the sestiere San Pol

Campiello della Scuola Grande di San Giovanni Evangelista and the church of San Giacomo di Rialto.

tico is a large distinctive *clock*, also 15th-century, and small Gothic tabernacle with a charming statue of a *Mado na and Child*.

CHURCH OF SANTA MARIA GLORIOSA DEI FRARI

Santa Maria Gloriosa dei Frari, a Franciscan church, was b gun in 1250 apparently to plans by Nicola Pisano. It was e larged and modified in 1338 by Scipione Bo Romanesque-Gothic in style, the **facade** is divided in three parts by pilasters, with spires at the top. A statue b Alessandro Vittoria is set above the portal while the figur at the sides are by the School of Bon.
The **campanile** is next in height to that of San Marco ar was built by the Celega in the 14th century. The **interior** the church is Latin-cross in plan with twelve columns su porting tall arches set between the nave and the two sic aisles. After the *Mausoleum of Titian*, note should be take of the many fine works which enrich the church and mak it perhaps the most famous place in Venice, after San Ma co, and together with San Zanipolo the one containing th greatest number of the mortal remains of famous men. the right aisle the *altar* by Longhena has two statues b Giusto Le Court; in the second bay is *Titian's tomb* (the arti died of the plague in 1576), made in 1852 by pupils of A tonio Canova. The third altar has sculpture by Alessand Vittoria. To the right of the right transept is the *Monumer to Admiral Jacopo Marcello*, by Pietro Lombardo. On th wall next to it is the *Monument to the Blessed Pacifico* wit a fine bas-relief (the *Baptism of Christ*) by Bartolo an Michele da Firenze. In the **Sacristy** there is a stupendou triptych by Giovanni Bellini depicting the *Enthrone Madonna and Child with Music-making Angels and Sain*

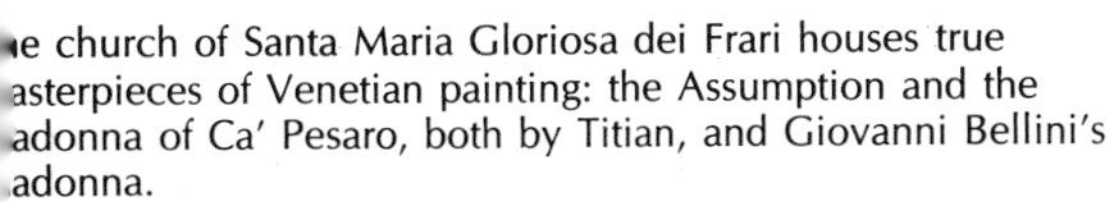

ıe church of Santa Maria Gloriosa dei Frari houses true
asterpieces of Venetian painting: the Assumption and the
adonna of Ca' Pesaro, both by Titian, and Giovanni Bellini's
adonna.

ı488). In the third chapel of the right apse is a *triptych* by artolomeo Vivarini.

he *Monument to Doge Francesco Foscari*, by the Bregno rothers (circa 1475), is in the chancel; on the left wall is ıe *Monument to Doge Nicolò Tron* by Antonio Rizzo. Be-ind the high altar rises the famous *Assumption* by Titian ı518). Of note in the first apse chapel to the left is a lovely *ladonna and Child* (1535) by Bernardo Licinio. In the third hapel is an altarpiece by Alvise Vivarino and Marco Basaiti vith *St. Ambrose Enthroned*. In the fourth, particular atten-on goes to a *triptych* by Bartolomeo Vivarini and a *St. John aptist* by Jacopo Sansovino on the baptismal font.

ı the left aisle, on the second altar, is the *Madonna di Casa 'esaro*, an altarpiece by Titian (1526) with, further on, the *lonument to Doge Giovanni Pesaro*, by Longhena (1669) nd the *Mausoleum to Antonio Canova*, planned by the ıaster and executed by his pupils.

EL DOGE

SCUOLA GRANDE
DI SAN ROCCO

nte dei Frari, Campo San Tomà, Ponte Storto with Rio San
vestro (the house of Bianca Cappello can be seen in the
ckground) and Campo San Stin.

SCUOLA GRANDE DI SAN ROCCO

All the most famous architects of the time had a hand in building of the Scuola Grande di San Rocco, erected tween 1515 and 1560. These included Bartolomeo E who designed it, Sante Lombardo, Scarpagnino, and fin Giangiacomo dei Grigi responsible for the finish touches. The results of this composite work owe much the style of Scarpagnino, who also created the f pedimented portal and the magnificent staircase in ground floor hall. Otherwise the **interior** is a monumen the art of Jacopo Tintoretto — whose original decoratio still in place — with his breathtakingly beautiful cycle paintings. The decoration of the Hostel began in 1564; the Great Hall the artist painted twenty-one canvases for ceiling in panels. Eight large canvases, painted betw 1583 and 1587, are in the large ground floor hall, divi by two rows of Corinthian columns into three aisles. Titia *Annunciation* is particularly lovely. The **Chancell Office** also has an *Ecce Homo* attributed to Titian an *Saint Rocco* by Bernardo Strozzi.

The facade of the Scuola Grande di San Rocco and, below, the church of the same name.

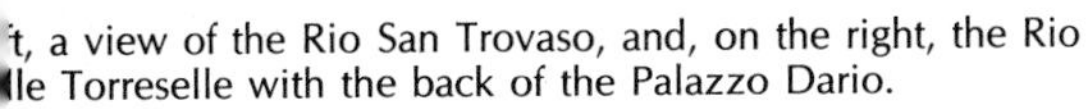

't, a view of the Rio San Trovaso, and, on the right, the Rio
lle Torreselle with the back of the Palazzo Dario.

e facade of the church of Santa Maria della Visitazione,
gun in 1493 and terminated in 1524, is attributed to Mauro
lussi and also to Tullio Lombardo.

HURCH OF SAN ROCCO

ıe church of San Rocco is right next to the Scuola Grande.
was rebuilt by Scalfarotto in the 18th century on the old
enaissance church. The **facade**, which echoes the motives
the Scuola, is decorated with statues by Morlaiter and
archiori and has a fine portal with a gable.
ıe **interior**, with a single nave and side chapels and a
ome over the sanctuary, houses a series of works by Tin-
retto — two of the most outstanding are *St. Rocco Healing
e Plague-stricken* and *St. Rocco in the Desert* —, by Porde-
one, *St. Martin and St. Cristopher*, and fine frescoes. The
lics of the Saint are in the sanctuary in an urn with a statue
St. Rocco above.

CHURCH OF SAN TROVASO

« *Trovaso* » is the contraction in dialect of Gervasio and P
tasio. The Church of San Trovasio, already extant in
11th century, was damaged by fire and rebuilt in 1590
classical forms with two tiers of pilasters on the **facade**
The Latin-cross **interior** has a nave only and contains imp
tant works by Pietro Lombardo, Domenico Tintoret
Michele Giambono, Jacopo Tintoretto, Palma Giovane a
Rosalba Carriera.

The church and the "squero" of San Trovaso.

?UERO OF SAN TROVASO

ear the **Church of San Trovaso** is the *squero* or private ckyard for the construction of ships, also called San ovaso.

e picturesque group of buildings, some of which are in ick and some of wood, faces on the rio with a landing for launching and the beaching of small vessels. It is here fact that new gondolas are built and repairs are carried t. This is the only one of the many squeri once active in city which still continues the centuries-old tradition of ipbuilding in the field of the typical Venetian craft.

e squero dates to the 17th century and the layout is basilly still what it was, despite periodical renovation, with its all juxtaposed buildings, some serving as workshops, me as dwellings. A characteristic feature are the small uses on the landing with wooden balconies and railings d roofing supported by poles.

IE GONDOLA

e history of this slender boat, traditionally used by the vellers of the lagoon, is a thousand years old. Said to date the times of the first doge in the 7th century, the gondola actually nominated for the first time in a public document 1094. The origin of the name itself is uncertain and may, ther symbolically, come from the Greek *kondyle*, or hell », or from *kondoura*, a sort of vessel, or from the Latin *mbula*, or « small boat ». The gondolas built by the Venen master hewers according to a tradition that was handed wn orally were not always as they are today. Those picted in 15th and 16th-century paintings were flatter ttomed and the stern and prow were not as high. The anking was brightly painted and decorated with costly pliqués, and the various noble families vied with each her in showing off their wealth. The two parts of the boat ere the craftsmen's fancy was given free rein were the ow, rather like a halberd with six teeth (one for each sesere in Venice), and the volute of the stern. In the 18th cenry the gondola was standardized (once some were larger, opelled by several oars) and it is now 10.75 m. long and 75 m. wide. The flat-bottomed boat is asymmetrical beuse it is propelled by a single oar on the starboard side.

e gondolier, whose « uniform » consists of a striped jersey d a beribboned straw hat, was once much more curiously d elegantly outfitted. Standing on a small platform in the rn he pushes the gondola with his single long oar which sts on the typically curved rowlock or *forcola*. Ever since 62 when the Senate of the Serenissima emanated a cree that put an end to the ostentatious ornamentation in hich one family tried to outdo the other the gondolas have en black. The only space left for decorative invention is the panels which cover the prow, sometimes carved with ant scrolls or — more rarely — with detailed views of the goon. Nor does the *felze*, a moveable arched shelter that rmed a sort of cabin at the center of the boat to shield the ssengers in bad weather, still exist. This hood, consisting black cloth ornamented with cords and ribbons, had tiny indows and a small shuttered door.

e gondolas which now ply the Venetian waterways, bareone twentieth of those there in the 18th century, are built d repaired at the Squero di San Trovaso, where the artins still keep the ancient craft alive.

CANAL AND ISLAND OF THE GIUDECCA

The entrance to the Giudecca Canal is right across from tl island of San Giorgio. For centuries the canal has been tl center for commerce and maritime trade in Venice and st today it is a large port where passenger ships dock. Its 1,6(meters wind along the embankments of the Giudecca i land, one of the most fascinating places in Venice where tl true soul of the city is still alive, both in the architecture ar in the trading activities. The mixture of ancient houses ar small palaces in a variety of styles alternating with war houses where modest artisans ply their trade gives meanir to what can then be encountered, on a larger scale, in tl city. The island and its structures are, in a sense, the essen(of Venice, a fragment of the city separated from its nucle by a strip of sea. Outstanding among the more importa buildings are the unusual silhouettes of the former **Stucl Mill**, the ex-**Church of SS. Cosma e Damiano** and, abov all, the churches of the **Zitelle** and of the **Redentore**, fine e amples of the sculptural quality of the Baroque. Original this small island went by the name of Spinalonga, and it w later called Giudecca, probably on account of the larg number of Jews who settled here (14th-15th cent.), but th is no more than a hypothesis. It was once much smaller b as time went by reclamation and consolidation of the lan turned it into what it is now.

Two pictures of the church of San Giorgio Maggio

Exterior of the church of San Barnaba.

A view of the canal of the Giudecca.

HURCH OF SAN GIORGIO MAGGIORE

an Giorgio Maggiore is one of Andrea Palladio's finest orks (1565-1580). The church was completed, in line with e original design, by Simeone Sorella in 1610.
he **facade** is tripartite with columns and Corinthian capi-ls. The statues of *St. George* and *St. Stephen* are set into e two niches between the columns. In the wings are the *usts of the Doges Tribuno Memmo* and *P. Ziani*, by Giulio al Moro. The **campanile** of 1791 is by Benedetto Buratti nd was built to replace the one that fell in 1773.
he inverted Latin-cross interior has a nave and two aisles nd a dome. Two splendid works by Tintoretto, a *Last Sup-er* and the *Gathering of the Manna*, are in the sanctuary. the apse are fine wooden *choir stalls* of 1598 carved by e Flemish sculptor Van der Brulle.

IORGIO CINI FOUNDATION

he former **Benedictine monastery on the island of San iorgio**, dating far back in time, was restored and in 1957 ecame the headquarters of the Giorgio Cini Foundation, ne of the most prestigious centers of culture and art in the orld, the setting for innumerable international congresses nd even summit meetings of heads of state. The monastery, nbelievably beautiful in the perfection of its Palladian ar-hitecture, includes among its many works of art a *Marriage f the Virgin* by Tintoretto. Of particular note among the oundation's various activities is that of the Centro di Cul-ra e Civiltà with various institutes which also boast a rich brary of incunabula, illuminated manuscripts, and a host f old drawings.

MUSEUMS AND GALLERIES

GALLERIA DELL'ACCADEMIA

For a general view of the development of Venetian painting in the five centuries ranging from the 14th to the 18th century a visit to the Academy Gallery is essential. It was officially created as an « Accademia dei pittori e scultori » by a decree of the Republic of Venice on September 14, 1750. The first director was Giambattista Piazzetta and the headquarters were in the building which currently houses the Capitaneria di Porto. In 1807 it was decided to move it to the buildings of the Church of Santa Maria della Carità, the Scuola Grande of the same name, and the Monastero dei Canonici Lateranensi, forming the new « Accademia delle Belle Arti ». The old **Scuola della Confraternita** had been completed between the 14th and the 15th centuries. The facade was now renovated by Maccarozzi in neoclassic style on a project by Giorgio Massari. The **Church of Santa Maria della Carità** was on the site of a precedent Romanesque structure; the workshop of Bartolomeo Bon was involved in the new structure which dates to between 1441 and 1452. The third building, the **Convent of the Lateran Canons**, is one of the finest examples of Palladian architecture in Venice. These buildings were adapted to their new function by Antonio Selva who had what was left of the Corinthian atriu and the short sides of the cloister torn down, replacing the with a double loggia so as to connect the rooms of the co vent with those of the church.
The original core of the present collection dates to the 18 century and was comprised of the paintings submitted b the aspiring academicians. From the time of its refoundir one donation followed the other, both by private individ als — in particular the Contarini bequest of 1838 and th Renier legacy of 1850 — and the « forced » donations of th religious institutions repressed by Napoleon, as well as a ditions, in more recent times, due to acquisitions on the pa of the State. An important group of paintings, chosen b Peter Edwards, president of the old Accademia from 179 1796, was bought in 1812. Works by Carpaccio, the Bel nis, Titian, Pordenone, and Paolo Veronese were acquire in the years immediately after. When Napoleon fell, th

Francesco Guardi: The Island of San Giorgio Maggiore.

ɔuvre had to return works by Paris Bordone, Jacopo Tin-
retto, and the *Supper in the House of Levi* which Paolo
eronese had painted in 1537 for the Refectory of the Con-
ənt of Santi Giovanni e Paolo.
s already stated, the rooms provide a complete panorama
Venetian painting, beginning with works still of Byzan-
ne inspiration. This period, up to the 14th century, is well
presented by examples which include polyptychs by the
eneziano's — Catarino's *Coronation of the Virgin* dating to
375, and the *Annunciation, Saints and Prophets* by Loren-
o of 1357. There are also works by Iacobello del Fiore, Ia-
obello Alberegno and Nicolo di Pietro.
ne 15th century is also represented by outstanding paint-
gs, including Giovanni Bellini's *Madonna and Child beveen St. Catherine and the Magdalen, Enthroned Madonna
doring the Sleeping Child in her Lap*, and the entire cycle
the *Legend of St. Orsola* by Carpaccio, originally painted
r the oratory of the Scuola di Sant'Orsola. There are also
umerous works by Vivarini, G. D'Alemagna, Lazzaro
astiani.

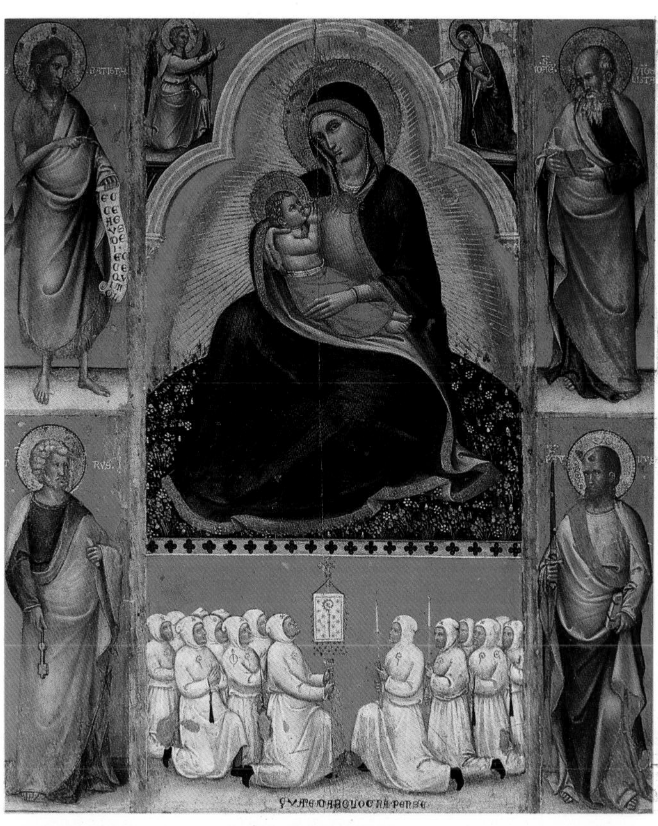

Giovanni da Bologna: Madonna of Humility.

Paolo Veneziano: Madonna Enthroned.

ccolò di Pietro: Enthroned Madonna and Child with Patron.

ɪrenzo Veneziano: Polyptych with the Annunciation
ɪd four Saints.

ɪiovanni Bellini: Pietà.

Gentile Bellini: Healing of Pietro de' Ludovici.

Giorgione (Giorgio da Castelfranco): The Tempest.

onifacio de' Pitati: The Rich Man's Feast.

ndrea Mantegna: St. George.

alma il Vecchio: Assumption.

the 16th century of particular note is Giorgione's most ous painting, *The Tempest*, as well as what remains of fresco showing a *Nude* that originally decorated the fa-e of the Fondaco dei Tedeschi. Then there is Titian's *Pie-*nd his *Presentation of the Virgin in the Temple*, Paolo onese's *Supper in the House of Levi* and his *Madonna Child with Saints*, as well as the stupendous *Miracle of Mark* and *Adam and Eve* by Jacopo Tintoretto. There is) a rich assortment of works by minor artists, Boccacci- Lorenzo Lotto, Paris Bordone, Schiavone, Pordenone. rks by Bernardo Strozzi, *Banquet in the House of the risee* and *Saint Jerome*; the *Parable of the Good Samari-* by Domenico Fetti; Mazzoni's *Annunciation*, as well as ntings by Marrei and others cover the 17th century.
18th century is particularly well represented, with some he most important works of Venetian artists, including tro Longhi's *Philosopher*, the *Fortune-teller* and a *cifixion* by G. B. Piazzetta, *Portrait of a Young Man* and *elf-Portrait* by Rosalba Carriera, *St. Joseph with the Child other Saints* by G. B. Tiepolo, and finally Canaletto's *ticato*.

aletto: Portico

n: Pietà.

oretto (Jacopo Robusti): Saint Mark Saves a Saracen.

On the following pages, Paolo Veronese: Feast in the House of Levi, detail of the left and of the right side.

FECIT D. COVI. MAGNV. LEVI
A. D. MDLXXIII.

LVCAE CAP. V.
DIE . XX . APR .

ɿentile Bellini: Miracles of the Holy Cross,
ʼhe Holy Cross Fallen into the Canal of San Lorenzo.

ʼittore Carpaccio: the Healing of a Lunatic.

Vittore Carpaccio: Legend of Saint Orsola (detail). The English Ambassadors Presenting the Proposal of Marriage to King Maurus of Brittain.

On the following pages: Vittore Carpaccio, Legend of St. Orsola (detail). Left to right: Hereus Takes Leave of his Father; Hereus Meets Orsola; Homage of Hereus to King Maurus of Brittain.

VICTORIS

Rosalba Carriera: Self-portrait.

G. B. Piazzetta: The Fortune-teller.

ancesco Guardi: Fire at S. Marcuola.

Pietro Longhi: The Chemist.

The ball-room with frescoes by G. Crosato.

MUSEO DEL SETTECENTO VENEZIANO

The Museum of the Venetian Eighteenth Century is in **Palazzo Rezzonico** in the sestriere of Dorsoduro.
In 1935 the palace was bought by the City of Venice which restored and refurbished the interior as a splendid aristocratic Venetian 18th-century home.
The **Ballroom** — entrance to which is via a *staircase* by G. Massari — with stupendous carved furniture by Brustolo leads to the **Room of the Allegory of Marriage**, named aft the fresco by Tiepolo depicting the *Wedding of Ludovic Rezzonico*, from the **Room of the Pastels** with works b Rosalba Carriera, to the **Hall of Tapestries**, with 17th century Flemish *tapestries*; from the **Throne Room**, former nuptial chamber with a fresco by Tiepolo, to the Hall ded cated to him where he painted the large fresco with *Fortur* and *Wisdom*: from the **Library Hall** with *canvases of myth*

ne Sala dei Pastelli and the Sala degli Arazzi.

The Salone del Brustolon and the Sala del Tiepolo.

Pietro Longhi: The Dancing-lesson: Venetian Masks; The Rhinocerous and the Promenade in the Piazza.

logical subjects* by Maffei to the **Sala del Lazzarini** and that of Brustolon with beautiful pieces of inlaid furniture made by the master from Belluno who was particularly active in Venice.

On the second floor the **Portego dei Dipinti**, with works by Piazzetta, Jan Liss and Giuseppe Zais, leads to the **Sala del Longhi** with 34 pictures of *life in Venice*. The *ceiling* is by Tiepolo. After two smaller rooms, frescoed by Guardi, comes the perfect reconstruction of an 18th-century bedroom. Two more small rooms, and the visitor finds him-

Room of the Green Lacquers known also as Salotto Calbo-Crotta.

self in a reconstruction of the villa at Zianigo with frescoes by Gian Domenico Tiepolo.
Of particular interest on the second floor are the **Room of the Clowns**, the **Chapel** frescoed by Tiepolo in 1749, and the **Sala del Ridotto** (Gaming room) with the famous small paintings by Guardi, the *Parlatorio delle Monache* (*Nuns' Parlor*) and the *Sala del Ridotto*. The small **Room of the Stuccoes** is particularly charming. Just as interesting on the third floor is the reconstruction of an old pharmacy or Chemist's Shop and a Marionette Theater, with a collection of 18th-century Venetian marionettes.

GALLERIA FRANCHETTI

The collection is situated on the upper floors of the **Ca' d'Oro**, and to get there one must first cross a fine courtyard — entrance to which is from the Grand Canal, through a lovely Gothic four-light opening — embellished by a 15th-century marble *well-head* before climbing an open staircase resting on Gothic arches. The ground floor portico is surrounded by various Roman and Hellenistic *statues* and has a mosaic pavement. The **Quadreria** (Picture Gallery) displays works by Antonio Vivarini, Vittore Carpaccio, Paris Borbone, Alessandro Vittoria, Titian, Mantegna — his splendid painting of *St. Sebastian* —, Van Dyck, Pontormo, Filippo Lippi, Francesco Guardi, Luca Signorelli, Van Eyck, Tintoretto, Sansovino. The Gallery now also contains the frescoes by Campagnola and Pordenone which were removed from the walls of the cloister of Santo Stefano, as well as old Venetian ceramics from the 11th to the 18th centuries including the famous fragments of the Conton collection.
Other rooms annexed to the Gallery belong to the Palazzo Giusti, which is next to the Ca' d'Oro. These three rooms contain bronzes of Venetian school and other examples of Flemish and Dutch art. Note should be taken in passing from the first to the second floor of the Ca' d'Oro of a splendid carved wooden *staircase*, originally in the Agnello House.

rancesco Guardi: Piazzetta S. Marco (Galleria Franchetti).

Francesco Guardi: Grand Canal with the church of the Salute (Galleria Franchetti).

PINACOTECA QUERINI STAMPALIA

The Querini Stampalia Collection of Paintings is housed i the palace of that name behind the Church of Santa Mar Formosa, next to the rich private library donated to the ci by Count Querini Stampalia.
The Picture Gallery consists of twenty rooms, on the secon floor, which contain furniture, porcelains, arms and music instruments as well as works by artists active between th 14th and 18th centuries.
The most interesting paintings include a *Self-Portrait* an *Adam and Eve* by Palma Giovane, the *Conversion of S Paul* by Andrea Schiavone, an *Adoration of the Madonna* b Lorenzo di Credi, a *Sacra Conversazione* by Palma Vecchi *Hunting in the Valley* by Pietro Longhi — the museum owr a rich collection of works by this artist —, various lanc scapes by Marco Ricci, the *Portrait of G. Querini* by G. I Tiepolo and a *Madonna and Child* by Bernardo Strozzi. Various rooms in the gallery still have their original 18tl century furnishings, with splendid Chinese lacquer furn ture, Louis XVI mirrors, stucco decoration. Also to be note are drawings by Giovanni Bellini, Titian, Raphael, Tintore to and Veronese.

Exterior of Palazzo Querini-Stampalia.

Palazzo Querini-Stampalia: the Green Drawing-room, in Venetian Baroque style of the 18th century.

Gabriele Bella: The Feast of the Thursday before Lent in Piazzetta San Marco.

Gabriele Bella: Women's Regatta on the Grand Canal.

Anonymous 17th-century painter: Allegory of the Holy Alliance (Museo Correr).

Vittore Carpaccio: The Visitation (Museo Correr).

MUSEO CIVICO CORRER

The Museo Civico Correr is situated in the **Napoleonic Wing of the Procuratie Nuove**. Formed around an original nucleus of paintings given in 1830 by the Venetian patrician Teodoro Correr, until 1922 it was installed in Palazzo Correr on the Grand Canal.

The entire conspicuous patrimony of the Correr collection has been divided into three sections, two of which are installed elsewhere: the Museum of the Venetian Eighteenth Century (Settecento) in Ca' Rezzonico and the Archaeological Museum in another wing of the Procuratie Nuove with an entrance from the Piazzetta. The Museo Correr is dedicated to the Historical Collections, the Picture Gallery and the Museum of the Risorgimento.

The **Historical Collections** are spread out over thirty-three rooms, on the first floor, in which an astounding variety of objects is on display, furnishing as complete a picture as possible of the social life, the institutions of art and history of the Most Serene Republic. Included in this wide array of precious objects are various representations of the Lion of St. Mark, symbols and banners of the Serenissima, coats of arms and portraits of the doges, their seals, the costumes of the doge and other high magistrates, depictions of public ceremonies, mementos of the famous plot of Bajamonte Tiepolo, an important coin collection, illustrations of ships and naval documents, keepsakes of the Battle of Lepanto, nautical maps and navigator's instruments, the map of the colonial conquests, weapons, flags, coats of arms, staffs of command and trophies, as well as Antonio Canova's early masterpiece, *Daedalus and Icarus*.

The **Picture Gallery** (**Quadreria**) is installed in nineteen rooms on the second floor. In the first and second of these are examples of Venetian-Byzantine art and works by 16th-century Venetian painters; outstanding is Paolo Veneziano. The third room features the works of Lorenzo Veneziano while of particular note in the next room dedicated to flamboyant Gothic are the 14th-century panels and the sculpture by Jacopo delle Masegne.

The fifth room contains Late Gothic Venetian painting which reappears in the sixth room featuring works by Jacobello del Fiore and Michele Giambono.

The greatest masterpieces of the Ferrarese artist Cosme Tura (note the splendid *Pietà*) are collected in the seventh room which also contains works by other artists from Ferrara and two *Madonnas* by Bartolomeo Vivarini. The following rooms are dedicated to Venetian wood sculpture and works by artists of the Flemish school including an *Adoration of the Magi* by Pieter Bruegel. Further on, one of the rooms has a *Pietà* by Antonello della Messina, a *Crucifixion* by Hugo van der Goes and a *Madonna and Child* by Bouts. Cranach, Bruyn and il Civetta are present in the twelfth room while the following room boasts paintings by Giovanni, Jacopo and Gentile Bellini. Alvise Vivarini and the artists close to him appear in the fourteenth room. Vittore Carpaccio's *Courtesans* and other works by the same artist cover the space of two rooms while the seventeenth contains Lorenzo Lotto's *Madonna and Child Crowned by Angels*. In the eighteenth are to be found examples of the work of the famous « Madonneri », Greek-Venetian painters of the 16th and 17th centuries. Examples of 16th-century ceramics are on exhibit in the last room of the Picture Gallery. Particularly admired is the famous « Correr dinner service » consisting of seventeen pieces decorated by Niccolo Pellipario in 1525.

Grevembrock: Glass-blower of Murano (Water-color,
iblioteca del Museo Correr).

MURANO

This typical settlement in the lagoon spreads out over f islands and was created by refugees from Opiterga and A no fleeing from the Huns and Lombards. It developed rap ly and as early as 1275 was already governed by a Veneti podestà but with regulations of its own. For centuries it w considered the vacation site for the patrician families Venice, and as a result churches and palaces were built a rebuilt.
Glass making, for which Murano has become famo throught the world, has ancient beginnings. In 1292 all glass factories of Venice were transferred to Murano so as protect the city from the danger of fire. With the affirmati of blown glass and the development of other techniques su as milk glass, Murano reached its zenith in the 15th centu Only a few of the many outstanding palaces are cited. T **Palazzo Da Mula**, a fine Gothic building, stands next to **Ponte Vivarini**; the **Palazzo Trevisan**, attributed to Palladio, no less interesting. On the opposite shore is the **Museo d l'Arte Vetraria**, or Glass Museum, in the former **Palaz Giustinian**. Of particular interest are the churches: the most mous is **SS. Maria e Donato**. The Basilica, which may ha been built in the 7th century by refugees from Altino, w rebuilt as it is now in the 12th century. In 1529 the chur of **Santa Maria degli Angeli** was rebuilt next to the **Monaste** of the same name to which it was attached. The **Church San Pietro Martire** in its present form dates to 1511. T square campanile is of 1502.

Glass-blowing in Murano.

The apse of the church of SS. Maria e Donato.

JRANO

ie original settlement of Burano was on a different island, oser to the sea, and it was probably due to some natural ılamity that the community of Burano later moved to « *Vi-ıs Buranis* », on the island near Mazzorbo. Life on the is-nd, which counted about 8,000 souls, was bound to Tor-ello up to the 18th century, when Torcello went into its fa-l decline. Life on Burano was always characterized by its lation with art. The musician B. Galuppi was born here in 706 and it was a fertile point of encounter for painters ove all in the 20th century.

ie most important economic activity of Burano is a felici-us encounter of art and craft: the lace which reached its enith between the 16th and 17th centuries, thanks also to e protection granted by the Dogaresses Giovanna Duodo ıd Morosina Morosini. There was a decline in lace-making the 18th century until a school was established in the 380s and 90s.

ıere are two churches on the island, **San Martino** founded the 16th century which contains the relics of the patron iints and martyrs Martin and Hadrian, as well as other markable works of art and furnishings, and the church of **anta Maria delle Grazie**, set on the site of a chapel of Doge rimani. It was closed as a church in 1810 and is now used a social center.

ie famous lace of Burano.

typical corner of Burano.

TORCELLO

Torcello is one of the loveliest islands in the lagoon thanks to its aura of times past.
It was one of the most important islands in the history of the early settlements and became bishop's seat in the 7th century when it had a much larger population than the barely hundred souls who live there now.
In 1247 Torcello had its own statute and a podestà, trade was lively and churches and palaces were being built. The malaria which spread as the result of the deviation of the mouth of the Stile marked the end of life on the island.
The **Cathedral of Santa Fosca** is a building of the year thousand which betrays the influence of Ravenna in its octagonal ground plan with a portico on five sides. The Greek-cross interior is highly impressive. The **Cathedral of Santa Maria Assunta** was founded in 639 and partly rebuilt in 1008, and is the finest example of the artistic influence of Ravenna, through which Byzantine art arrived in the lagoon. Inside is a 12th-13th-century Venetian-Byzantine mosaic, with the *Last Judgement*; the *iconostasis* or rood screen with marble columns and thirteen *icons* of the early 15th century; the altar with a *Roman sarcophagus* from Altino under the altar table, and a *Madonna and Child*, a 13t century mosaic in Venetian style, while the *Apostles* a 12th-century Ravennate in style. The *crypt* dates to the 9 century. These are the most important works in tl cathedral. Behind the church is the **Chapel of San Mar** where it is said the relics of the Evangelist stopped on the way to Venice. Little remains of the **Baptistry** that on stood facing the church. Archaeological finds and eviden of the history of Torcello and the lagoon as well as wor of art and paintings are installed in the **Museo dell'Estuar** in the **Palazzo del Consiglio** and in the **Palazzo dell'Arch vio** (which also has paleo-Veneto, Etruscan, and Gre finds); both dating to the 14th century. Only a few vestig of the **Palazzo del Podestà** are still extant (plaques, coats arms, column fragments).

The cathedral of Torcello dedicated to S. Maria Assunta.

A typical canal and the church of S. Fosc

CONTENTS